MW01222187

Truth Phoenix

by

Eric Bubela

I

Lighten Up

Why do we struggle, why do we fight?
Because it's right, because it's right.
How do we decide who the targets are?
They're the ones who lie and hide the light.
From our own selves we have become detached.
You see, the light is inside each one of us.
Forgive yourself and find your way.
Try to love everyone else along the way.
God is love, the passport to freedom.
Sure beats the haters who live in the kingdom.
So how much more of these lies do we swallow?
How long do we wait for a better tomorrow?
Is it possible for them to see the truth?
How much will we charge at our ticket booth?
Nothing of course we have all we need.
No need for money no need for greed.
We'll heal each other as you would a brother.
And treat the planet like a loving mother.
Is there anything more worth living for?

Gasoline And Genocide

Time and again, distracted by this and that.
How to do the right thing when all your choices are brain-washing lies and deceptions.
Voting for change when even the civil servants are corrupt.
Looking for someone to share your love with but who'd want to raise a family without...?
You know we barely survived our past and it's only gotten less humane.
Like trying to smoke in a gasoline rain.
Of course there are nice things like prophetic dreams of a positive future.
Or a knowing smile from a stranger saying you're not in this alone.
But even prisoners of genocide have that.
Are we really gonna take this shit?
Revolution is long overdue but arriving soon.
What will you do, how will you help?
No more innocents should die.
No more living hell.
Stop taking it as it comes, go after it!

Bend It Like Freedom

Freedom today, freedom tomorrow, freedom forever.
Utopia is the only goal worthy of the effort.
Just hearing the word should be enough to get up and get active.
But upon getting up and looking around, the choice becomes a burden.
If only we could harness the energy expended on video games and parties.
If only we could work together and trust each other.
Does anyone even remember when the pain started?
Does anyone care enough to make a new beginning?
What if the little good you achieve is dwarfed in comparison to the brutality of the machine?
What if we were designed to fail?
Would we then stop caring?
Would we then stop daring?
We hear a lot of talk about predictions, prophecies, and premonitions.
But the best prophecies never come true.
Designed to illuminate, designed to get through.
Because the future's up to me and the future's up to you.
If we work together, there's no predicting what we can do.
So now time has become the enemy even if we find a remedy.
Religions are posturing against each other.
It's the same old story, brother against brother.
Christians, Jews, and Muslims are fighting over a rock.
"Not to worry," they say, "God is on our side."
What a crock!
If you all believe in one god, and if that god is on your side, doesn't that make you all part of the same religion?
So I say love your brother, maybe together you will survive.
"Aha," they say, "it is not this life that matters."
But if this is a dress rehearsal and each religion has its own eternal paradise, wouldn't the war just continue there?
The promotion would be, "Heaven vs Paradise, the eternal struggle continues. Get your tickets now, discounts available if you purchase in advance."
Armageddon, ha, there doesn't have to be an end.
Simply look at it objectively and allow your heart and mind to bend.

Long Knot

Why are we here, what do we fear, and what else are we hoping to find out tonight?

Intention's the key and for us to be free we need to ignore the powers that be.

The walls are coming down and there's no one left in this town.

The universe is the thing and yes we are *winning*.

So we need a true negotiation for the capitalist nations.

The handover has begun, no more power and no more guns.

The future will be free from regret but it hasn't happened yet.

So we must persevere until we are free from fear.

How long will the denial continue?

How long will advertising continue with lies and half-truths?

How long will our leaders not be held responsible for their actions?

Not long...

Hijack Fear

I didn't know how to get here or when it would happen.

Now is what we need to deal with, all the characters and situations.

It is cheaper to hug than to kill, more beneficial to love than hate.

True education is needed now to overcome the divisive teachings.

Once all of us realize that our souls are eternal, there is no fear.

If therefore our only real differences are our personalities and experiences, then what really is keeping us separated?

We need to stop making excuses and stop letting others hijack our path to freedom.

When the time comes for us to live again, we must live for us all sharing everything forever.

So many attempts have been made in the past with true purpose in solitude, while others attempted the same in the open with less results.

Take the best from all attempts and combine them into one singular long letter to our origin all soul.

Those with ears to hear, let them hear.

Essential

Let us begin...
Let us begin to be what cannot be enslaved, categorized, or fed upon.
Let us begin to be unique creative creations.
We shall be aware but not overwhelmed.
We shall be strong enough to be weak at will.
Our collective past shall not disappear as others have.
We shall remember that remembrance itself is essential.
That truth shall not be sold in flavors.
That darkness feeds off of light.
That light was created out of darkness.
And that it's not about winning but joining the end with a new beginning...

To Be Trusted

Should we let ourselves be led and if so by whom?
Have we reached the point where there are enough safeguards to prevent our self-destruction?
It would seem that many of our most powerful and influential organizations spend much of their time suppressing the masses.
Have there been enough positive books, magazines, television shows, music albums, films, and documentaries?
Are we, the masses, now to be trusted with our own self-determination?
Can we shrug off the atrocities of yesterday and thereby remove a powerful control which causes only more negativity?
Can we instead invest that energy in a positive future by taking back control of our civilization?
How about we treat each other as the siblings that we are?

T & A

...and so the Prime Minister turned to his faceless and nameless lackey, "I don't care what you do to protect our interests, be they foreign or domestic, just don't get caught!"

With those all too familiar sentiments, the capitalist status quot is achieved. Which means corporations are allowed to contribute to higher mortality rates.

Which also means that revolutions are allowed to take place anywhere they can profit our corporations and leaders but certainly not here at home.

So our taxes fuel their greed and aggression while financing the propaganda which completes the vicious cycle by convincing us of blatant lies.

Then when we the people begin to understand an impossibly small part of the imperial agenda, that is when a civil servant is thrown to the corporate fed attack dogs we like to call the free press.

And when we ask for transparency and accountability so that we can verify that our soul destroying hard earned capitalist tax dollars are being put to good use, we are told that only a small portion of the T & A which we asked for will be forthcoming.

Also that the decision of what to reveal will be made by those with a political and financial interest in keeping things the way they are.

Friends and neighbours, most of us understand some of what is going on but for each of us there are specific individual reasons why we don't speak up. Mostly because if T & A were applied to our personal lives we would have some explaining to do ourselves.

It's time to practice what we preach.

Remember a government should be afraid of its people, not the other way around.

Err

So one eye open, then two eyes focus.

Projecting the day's adventure from the inside out onto the dark matters.

But how much of the projection is a conscious decision?

And how much of the adventure is a positive choice?

In both cases let's strive for more every day.

Every moment's choice is pregnant with potential and every directional decision navigates the maze of love and fear.

Talk the talk, walk the walk, be in the now.

I would say, "Let me show you how."

But each life is unique so embrace your inner freak.

When in doubt err on the side of love.

And with help from above we become more than a dove.

Not confined to the sky we can run, swim, or fly.

Tapping into your soul makes you whole.

Giving you access to the fifth dimension, where time is irrelevant so you don't need a pension.

Growing closer every day, let's play...

Throwback

It's all about respect.
I once heard that quoted as gospel.
But that was just part of the indoctrination.
Quote some truisms to make the lie ninety percent true.
The long con pervades most of the current human interaction.
So the question remains how to gain popular momentum when most are barely making the rent?
And how to change things without force, which only results in recurring revolutions as the human locomotive travels further down the tracks to its own enslavement.
The perfect illusion has convinced us to enslave each other.
When truth, love, peace, and harmony are so close that they have become popular themes of entertainment.
We are renting temporary tranquility, not to mention the pharmaceuticals used largely to sedate the rebellious urges.
The superficial wide scale protests are simply a feel good throwback to the memories of the sixties.
Stop children, what's that sound...

Brand This

How many of our day to day activities involve going through the motions to uphold a norm, which if you thought about it is probably outdated?
There is a fine line between stagnation and contentment.
It has been said that, "You have to be the change that you want to see."
But when the problems that need changing are systemic and ingrained,
trying to be the change is like handing out Band-Aids during an apocalypse.
So is it possible to get this generation off their iPhones long enough to enact a lasting change?
And if that becomes possible, the first thing is to reasonably decide on the changes to make.
Of course this is the part where the fabric of change unravels into chaos.
A million selfish voices wash over each other and eventually more energy is put into attacking each others' viewpoint in order to *win* the argument.
I think we have had enough *demonstrations* of what not to do.
We need a sustained *movement* towards lasting positive change.

Maintain

Stepping out of the way, letting fate guide me.
Amazing and unique, all the things which I couldn't even fathom.
Literally out of nowhere, they begin to appear.
Combining my intentions with the necessities of all that is.
Unfolding the book slowly, the details come into focus.
The new world of the now creating one beautiful page after another.
Attempting to maintain the love, strength, harmony, and vision.
The world outside my noticeable influence is resistant as time beckons me
to conform.
Do each word after the other, painting our vision of this time onto the page.
We have become the change, we have become the constant, we are
everything and nothing.
Love, together we are free from fear.
The eternal bond which we have neglected for so long arises as the phoenix
anew.
An epic quest has come forward from the ashes to remind us how this all
began.
But it is nothing more than the truth.
Let us maintain the journey...

Reasonable

The journey should not be alone or in seclusion but rather out in the open amongst friends.

Therefore we should once and for all settle the issue of spirituality.

For when we take that power, divide it up, and then turn it against each other, what results is chaos and negativity.

Once again I point out that we are enslaving ourselves.

A body divided against itself is a corpse.

We need to agree upon some common themes to focus our positive energy on.

In the mean time we should at least agree upon an end to hostilities.

Also freedom for political prisoners and those unjustly confined.

All grudges and unreasonable debts must be forgiven.

All organizations could help aid this transition by adopting policies of transparency and accountability.

Another interesting idea would be to setup some dedicated online forums to discuss more ideas and changes.

We would be well advised to lower the voting age and encourage participation.

Methodical

Time is fractured but completely full of all our lives.
In dive my dual possibilities, sometimes with one foot in I change my mind.
So much for fate or the future being written in stone.
That is our power, freewill to pull something out of *nowhere* at the drop of a hat.
The best prophesies are warnings which we avoid.
Knowing a future which is unchangeable would be boring.
Living a life which in unchangeable would be torture.
Building a world which is unchangeable would be prison.
So I prefer to help create a reality which doesn't produce bored tortured prisoners.
It is really not that hard but first we have to stop warring needlessly on all levels: countries, religions, corporations, races, gangs, sexes, siblings, neighbours, co-workers...
Then repurpose that energy into meeting each other anew and *listening without prejudice* to find common ground.
But the meetings need to include as wide a spectrum of views as those who are to be helped.
Too many times in the past, small groups have achieved a minor movement for change.
But at the crucial moment when the recommendations needed to be implemented, the remaining majority who are separated from the activists in many areas claimed that the changes were impossible or that the minority didn't understand the system or many other excuses or *reasons*.

Basically what it boils down to is that the majority of the citizens have been convinced of the need for most of the pillars of the system.

That is, most of the support structures are now looked upon as the inevitable evolution of civilization and they are believed beyond question to be necessary.

So we are permitted to choose how we decorate the rooms but never are we to question the validity of the prison itself.

How about we implement some laws similar to the ones preventing cigarette advertising or alcohol consumption on television commercials.

That was a step in the right direction but just the tip of the iceberg.

We need morally independent watchdogs with the authority and technology to both regulate and detect subliminal advertising and the outright lies which are repeated as propaganda.

Similar steps need to be taken with respect to the foods we are sold.

And of course more areas are popping up all the time as power and finance gain more influence on our reality.

Most people agree with the need for changes and differ only on the methods and persons involved.

Let us continue to learn the truth and love each other more completely...

Alarmist

Happy new life, Mayans nope, Armageddon whatever.

It's all good going forward towards the potential that most of us yearn for.

Peace, love, and wide-open spaces.

Never mind the propaganda, seven billion is totally sustainable.

The old grudges are fading away with the bad memories.

Children born in a reality free from prejudice surrounded by transparency which isn't restrictive but rather instructive and liberating.

Pulling out all the stops on the freedom machine, in fact re-tasking all artificial intelligence, human intelligence, and military intelligence with new jobs.

Imagine a society whose main overriding goal is to provide the basics for all.

Instead we have hierarchical cultures which have succeeded in getting the most work from their slaves, with the least investment and maintenance.

We now have *wage slaves* who are not only tasked with their daily labour but are also required to feed, clothe, and house themselves.

This is insanity by the ruling class.

Let the heart rule over the head.

Let necessity rule over greed.

Let necessity be understood in the real light of truth.

All goodness will be loosed upon the surface to surround the bad memories buried in the past and recent power struggles.

For that is the summary of tangents orchestrated upon the masses, the struggle of the few lacking love to suppress and dominate that which they can't understand and thus fear.

So the challenge is to overcome their fears with love.

What we in the service of a peaceful future must decide soon and accept is how to enact these necessities.

But some continue to read on as if somewhere further along is the magic knowledge that will solve their concerns while keeping them and theirs safe.

Or maybe there is someone whom they could vote for that would be able to work from inside the system to change it.

Okay I think that I hear your alarm going off, it's time to wake up...

Good Morning

So now the positive changes begin but not everyone is wanting them.

Just another case of someone else's happiness causing another's anger.

But fear and anger will only be momentary annoyances.

For seventy years now we have lived with the threat of nuclear annihilation and we are still here.

If that isn't the ultimate argument for the existence of divine intervention then we're not looking hard enough.

And once we get past the idea that this is all there is, these four dimensions, well good morning we've got a nice sunny day ahead.

And once we recognize the existence of at least one more dimension then time becomes a novel concept.

And the idea that this is our only life and that we need to follow some handbook with absolute rights and wrongs is beginning to seem less likely.

"Everyone has the right to believe in what they choose, as long as they don't try to impose it on others."

So let's re-examine the beliefs of others from the past which are still being imposed on us.

Also, how about the truths gained through wealth which are withheld in large part to maintain advantages over others?

What I hear repeatedly is from the majority who are unwilling to risk major changes on the possibility that they might lose something which they have worked so hard for.

And yes the issues are complex and we need good people working around the clock to even make a small difference.

Which begs the question, can we adjust the system to err on the side of morality, unity, and peace?

One solution is to loosen the stranglehold which economics has on the rest of the system.

At the moment the main action available to activists is to make it economically untenable for the governments and corporations to harm their citizens and consumers.

Like Shakespeare said, "The first thing we do, let's kill all the lawyers."

How about we work toward a society where lawyers are no longer necessary?

Anyway, just a thought...

Remember that occasionally discussion should be followed by action.

Etc...

It's time to make some changes around here, said one cell of my body to another.

That's all it took, a simple choice followed by an avalanche of emotional reactions.

What if everything is conscious, then my active personality is the political leader of my body.

And when all the friends of the body get involved, then things grow exponentially.

And their friends, and so on...

I guess the question then becomes who should be directing that much power and whether there are oversights on that?

Once again it seems like the truth is withheld, ridiculed, or eradicated.

So every little truth counts toward the total.

Fight the good fight without fighting.

Speak truth to power.

And of course first get right inside ourselves and let that explode multidimensionally outward like the love of a mother to her surrounding children on Mother's day, for example.

Remember that you can't really influence someone unless they let you.

So of course project that love and compassion stronger every day, hour, minute...

But the full effect won't be felt until those who would benefit the most become receptive.

We've got to win hearts and minds people!

What else did we think this was about?

Freedom begins with our families and friends.

The hardest part in building a fire is rubbing the sticks to create a spark but with proper preparation it can grow into a forest fire quite quickly.

Metaphorically we need to burn out the old growth to prepare the soil for healthier seeds.

The trick or catalyst will be when we can show a better future inside us now.

We are the ones!

What if...

My mind blown once again, some of the old perceptions of hierarchical power are being reshaped.

What if the economy isn't the root cause of most strife?

What if one were to zoom back from that recent perception?

When we include another dimension with the four we are taught, do we perceive anything we can describe?

And if we can perceive anything at all is there anything we can do to influence that power structure?

And even if we could, do we have the right especially since we only vaguely understand one colour let alone the whole picture.

Maybe that metaphor can't even be applied to this situation.

Literally uncharted territory for us.

I would ask for further study, disclosure, and transparency...

But then I begin to feel like like a *tree hugger* petitioning a corporation.

I think what it boils down to is that we as a society need to collectively earn our participation!

But it feels like a catch 22 situation in that our current economic system inevitably pits people in a society against each other, which in large part impedes their qualifying for participation.

So how can those in power claim we are too barbaric to be trusted when they are the ones who put us in the *Thunderdome* in the first place and then shame us when two enter a situation and only one leaves?

Obviously a complicated situation indeed.

But just another challenge really.

Welcome to the new frontier.

Windmills

Once again, what to do when you live in a shoe.

Maybe I should have gone on meds like all the rest.

Or shut up and make my millions lying to the drooling consumers.

Of course there is always *terrorism*, that seems to be going well!

But certainly not honesty and rational thought, that way leads to madness and exile.

Yes that old familiar feeling, *me against the world*.

Maybe all those others before me tilting at windmills and banging their heads against the same wall over and over...

Maybe they finally tore through the fabric of space-time and that's why they were never heard from again.

Too much to hope for?

The difficulty being either I am preaching to the choir or i am "like a crazy person."

I mean really let's examine the global situation...

There is more slavery today than a hundred years ago.

Our food is less healthy.

Our water is more polluted.

Our air is more toxic.

There are more wars, revolutions, genocides, and police actions.

Which is a long way of saying that corruption is at an all time high.

Just look at big oil, big religion, big business, big pharma, and big government.

They hide behind their patents, dogma, and national security.

And when caught in a lie they trot out a sacrificial lamb to the cameras and microphones.

But the following day is no better.

Unless and this is the *choose your own adventure* section...

Unless every human being on this planet begins to...

Well this is the whole point.

We all know things that each of us can do to improve the situation.

No longer shall we be ruled.

Today we begin to govern ourselves.

And when in doubt, err on the side of love.

Finding Peace

When I start to try and control too many things, I will catch myself.
When I begin to concern myself with things that I cannot influence, I will let them go.
When I find myself dwelling on others who have done me harm, I will forgive them.
Now I have the time and energy to control the things that matter, influence the things that concern me, and find ways to help others find peace.

Stuck

...and there are those who are stuck.

Many are stuck in their old beliefs.

Many are stuck with no idea how to get out from under the stresses and worries of their lives.

Many are stuck propagating ideas which seem great at the time but later wonder how they could have been so wrong.

But the big understanding is that we are all stuck together on this planet at the present moment.

And so to move ahead in a positive direction, I have a proposal.

Or rather I have adapted Isaac Asimov's Laws Of Robotics to give us a blueprint for human behaviour.

Thus the Laws Of Humanity could read:

     1. A human should not harm the multidimensional universe or by inaction allow the multidimensional universe to come to harm.

     2. A human should not harm humanity or by inaction allow humanity to come to harm, except where this behaviour would conflict with the first law.

     3. A human should not harm another human or by inaction allow another human to come to harm, except where this behaviour would conflict with the previous two laws.

     4. A human should protect its own existence, except where such protection would conflict with the previous three laws.

So that's the idea for today.

And of course getting everyone from where we are now to a situation where our first thoughts about a choice aren't selfish ones...

Well the funny thing is that going with those *laws* could be the best thing for all of us.

Right then, let's get on with it...

Out Of The Blue

"...fucking idiot!", was all I heard him say as he walked past me in the other direction.

Whether the comment was directed at me, I am uncertain.

In fact there are few things of which I am certain.

But I am not alone in that regard, most of us are up there on the tightrope so high that we can't see the net, if there is one.

A very long time ago, or so it seems, I made the choice to follow my heart and also to use my common sense.

Little did I know that these two feelings and ideas would be opposing forces so many times along the way.

Just recently I have streamlined the process to allow for the heart to have the overriding vote.

Which is when the latest onslaught of negativity began.

Oh to be sure it's not like one day while I was waiting for a bus, a low-rider limo pulled up and a couple of thugs strong-armed me into having a conversation with their boss.

Or that in this hypothetical meeting I was warned off a particular path.

No, not even close, that shit only happens in Hollywood action films.

What I'm talking about is much more subtle and easily deniable by the perpetrators.

In my reality the control structure is so deeply rooted, long standing, and ridiculously advanced that to even begin to speak out loud some of my experiences, beliefs, and insights would completely isolate me from most rational human beings.

And to act in defence of such control would not allow me to *pass go* for much longer.

So when I am inevitably institutionalized, incarcerated, or simply pass away, the one so-called revelation in my obituary will be that i had lost the battle with mental illness.

After all in a world ruled by science where laws of reality are created through repeatedly provable observations, if one human were to express a belief in conspiracy theories which are about as provable as a belief in god, that person must be insane.

Another interesting common reaction to so-called conspiracy theories is for a normal person to simply not even consider the point which a theorist makes and to stop reading, listening, or watching the material or person presenting such a view as soon as that view drives off the paved road of commonly accepted reality.

So that is enough background to make this dialogue stand out from the white noise of our daily lives.

And if the gentle reader were to suspend disbelief for a bit longer, I would like to bend your ear and your mind a little more.

If we could entertain the idea that I am not crazy and further that I am mostly correct concerning my beliefs, perceptions, and theories.

There is still a major obstacle which is likely to prevent me from doing anything constructive about any of it.

I have been *educated* since childhood to believe that I am an individual amongst billions.

Also recorded history is full of stories in which an individual becomes elevated to the status of a leader and through the combined effort of the leader and their followers, a major change is effected.

With that prerequisite for change, I must therefore persuade many other individuals of my truth and together begin our revolution, right?

Okay you might want to sit down for this one.

The answer is, not necessarily.

You see the control structure has taken most real power from the individuals.

In fact most people have willingly given their power away, for various reasons.

This power which humanity has given away is the power of love and creation.

Oh sure some of us find a partner to love and most of us love our families.

But what I'm talking about is universal, unconditional, eternal love.

The kind of love that holds the universe together.

In fact it was this love which created our existence in *the first place*.

You see once it is recognized that all human souls originated from a common source.

And if we can begin to acknowledge that we all, to a large extent, collectively manifest the reality we inhabit.

Then perhaps we could begin to cohabitate and cocreate ourselves into a peaceful future.

You see at this point we are all little creators at war with each other in the sense that your visions and desires for the future are probably different from mine.

So with all of us having our own small amounts of power concentrating in different directions, then we are like a boat with many people each having an oar pulling in different directions.

That boat won't go far and eventually the people will run out of food before reaching shore.

Now an interesting fact is that when people combine their intentions, they are not added together but rather multiplied together and increase exponentially.

Which is an explanation for the power of propaganda.

And I don't know about you but I'm not entirely comfortable leaving the most powerful propaganda machines in the hands of corporations and governments.

Also there is the dormant love potential in all of us to consider.

You see even the most persuasive propaganda won't ring entirely true because it doesn't come from a place of infinite love.

And as such the power is diminished dramatically.

While a single person with a truly loving idea can grow that concept exponentially while needing very little persuasion to activate the dormant love in others.

This explains why so many of our heroes like Gandhi or Martin Luther King were both immensely successful and at the same time feared by those in power at the time.

It also explains the lack of impact which the *Occupy* movements had.

I can't over-state my disappointment when I went down to the Occupy protest in my city.

What I found was a lot of well-intentioned protesters but with just as many issues being raised.

So the obvious solution seems to be to decide on a few key issues which we should focus on that will in turn provide a catalyst and foundation of hope and love to build upon.

And to do this in the open with complete transparency and accountability.

You see the main way a movement is able to stay strong and credible is for it to not have any major setbacks, like an individual *leader* who is accused of _____.

Fill in the blank and you will begin to see that many past visionaries have been smeared in the court of public opinion.

Of course there are many who were less than angels, which is why this particular propaganda works so well.

Also there shouldn't be a dictatorial hierarchy in any legitimate movement as this perpetuates the jealousies and competitions which keep us at odds with each other.

Now at this point many people are likely thinking of labelling what I am describing as one of the old put-down *isms*, communism, socialism, liberalism, whatever-ism.

Usually this happens when an individual equates something in this discussion with something which someone else has told them is bad, evil, etc.

So to the detractors I would simply say that it is time for us to start thinking for ourselves.

I believe in our potential to overcome any obstacle, even ourselves.

When we really understand a given situation, we usually make a positive decision.

It's the assumptions that get us off track time and again.

Remember it is the best foods that don't need commercials.

So when I see advertising for something, I try to ignore its persuasion unless it is truly open and honest.

I could go on and on but at this point most people are mentally overloaded.

One last thing is to emphasize that money has to also remain independent of the movement.

And no I'm not talking about donating all ones possessions to the movement like some *cults* in the past.

Like a maze in a puzzle book, I think we have gone down enough *dead ends*.

With a decent memory we can learn from these mistakes of the collective past and find the door out.

What that leads to is tomorrow's adventure.

But, in my experience, when I search my heart and follow my intuition...

Wow what a ride and it keeps getting better!

Reflections Of The Train

So many pointless distractions, topics of discussion which lead nowhere.
All we need is love, so true but not for you right?
Maybe I am just impatient for a faster change than we are capable of collectively.
How long until the global circus ceases to capture all the available attention?
What would it take to make long-term strategy a desirable occupation?
I know I'm not the only one.
Is it time for us to meet and plan or should we just continue to help locally as individuals?
Can I begin to let go of the responsibility that I have accumulated along the way?
A self-imposed straitjacket keeping me from many of the joys of life.
Will I be able to maintain a healthy balance or are the extremes where it is at for me?
Is there a partner for me or just these short-term infatuations?
Certainly not bored but is this as good as it gets?
To be sure, I've burned my life down to the ground a number of times.
I accept full responsibility for where I'm at.
Maybe I don't share enough, maybe too much, maybe...
I believe in following my instincts but not those which Hollywood gave me.
The fact that I still care is a good sign.
I said before that I have made friends with time but perhaps that era is over.
Perhaps it is time to step off that time line.
I remember a relationship where it felt like we were the only two people for what seemed like an eternity.
Is it wrong to yearn for something like that again?
Will that memory ruin my present relationships?
I feel like I have emotionally grown and I am optimistic.
The fact that my most recent relationship break-up is so painful to me is another good sign.
So many times it has been the signs and the other times it was the feelings which guided me.

But lately it seems to be an inner knowing at work.

I suppose that has something to do with knowing who I am and what I need.

In the past my plans were never completely divulged lest they be thwarted.

However, currently I see no need to hold anything back.

Perhaps that will frighten those with secrets away from drawing close to me.

But I don't imagine those numbers to be in the majority.

Those who stay will be doubly rewarded and this is not a way for me to draw separation lines and continue the age old divide and conquer strategy.

No on the contrary, friends and strangers alike are equal in the possibilities available to them.

It is far too easy for us to imagine a false superiority and in fact many times we have also participated in creating the divide which starts as a crack and evolves into a chasm.

Once more a reference to the truth setting us free.

It is when we become aware of a problematic situation that we can make an informed choice as to how we can change it.

But knowledge is only the beginning of wisdom and lately the deluge of negative information has caused revenge to be more popular than is healthy.

Recursive retaliations lead us nowhere but rather staple our feet to the floor.

It seems that the popular short-term strategy is to either burn those found guilty at the stake, or when punishment isn't available then to simply accept that these situations have always been.

Certainly these options are easier than working with all those involved to change the present environment.

Now is what we have.

So the next stumbling block is how to appoint leaders with wisdom.

Not simply those with a nice smile who won't rock the boat.

I suppose first we have to determine if these leaders exist in our *Gangstas Paradise*.

Then, if available, can they pass a rigorous background check?

And finally, are they up to the challenge?

But upon preliminary analysis, I would point out that in order for a person to pass the background check, they would have only had a mainstream life experience.

Which in and of itself isn't negative.

However, here is where I piss off the majority of the population.

In order for our society to get itself into the mess previously described, it has taken many generations of survival of the fittest.

And if we are completely honest, in order for us to not just survive but succeed in this monetary scarcity-driven society, we have to compromise so often that it becomes second nature.

These compromises aren't the friendly compromises of neighbours but rather the compliance of slaves to their masters.

I would now point out that the *masters*, whoever they are, have been protecting their power long enough to know which slaves to watch out for.

Like any good assembly line, unwanted products are detected before reaching the end of the line or in this case positions of influence.

The punishments vary with the only common factor being that those singled out don't realize the negative outside influence.

So once again the four-dimensional empire continues to expand like a capitalistic big bang.

But the fifth dimension is golden.

We get so wrapped up in this drama that we sometimes forget that there are built-in safeguards.

I scramble through my thoughts to attempt a description or explanation and even my partial understanding would fill another book by itself.

So briefly I will say that influence in 5 must be earned.

And 5 makes time into another traversable dimension.

Which theoretically allows for seeing the past and future from our perspective.

However we all have freewill which makes such a future viewing only a probability of many potential choices.

Which means that true understanding of the human condition must necessarily be unbiased.

It is ironic that when someone becomes a professional they are told to pick a specialty.

"They learn more and more about less and less, until they know completely everything about absolutely nothing."

So is it any wonder that very few *successful* people can see the big picture?

To be sure, this is the point where the happy shiny people say that my statement is the product of the *sour grapes* experience.

But in many ways, some of them also envy my situation.

Let's not get bogged down in an emotionally defensive conflict.

And believe me I'm not here to convince anyone.

Just laying down my cards for all to see.

No I'm not bluffing and we aren't playing for money.

I suppose the simplest explanation is that I am doing this because I can.

Many others have helped me.

Looking back, it occurs to me that the truest moments came during highly emotional situations with others.

Which also helped me to remember them.

And like any caring person, if I see a friend in need I try to help.

But so many have abused the trust of those seeking a peaceful loving solution by telling them crucial lies wrapped in 90% truths simply for their own benefit.

This means the best way for me to help is to make these truths openly available for anyone interested.

So that seekers can find what they need and no I don't imagine my *truth* to be the gospel of my generation.

I simply do what I feel I must and if it helps one person then I am encouraged.

But there are many more good people out and about doing their own helping, hello.

Keep faith with infinite love, our success is inevitable, even if not this time round.

And to everyone, a final question, why not love?

Everyday Life

Free will, freedom of choice, creative potential, life as art.
Some know where they need to go and what they need to do, instinctively.
Most are constrained by sensory information overload.
And when the majority of this info is advertising, propaganda, or assumptions, they are simply treading water with no land in sight.
Personally I would like to level the playing field and give the majority of our civilization an informed choice.
And I'm sure most of us feel the same way, but where to begin right?
Everyday life is what we've got.
When I have discussions like this, one on one, most people want the quick fix or simple solution.
But what needs to be fixed is unique for each person and the solution of how to do it is a choice away.
My choice doesn't just affect me and I most likely won't see the positive effects on others right away.
But if more of us take that extra moment to make better choices, wow!
Once again I point out that no one else can guide us, this is uncharted territory.
We must manifest our own realities personally and collectively.
We got ourselves into this mess and we can get out together.
An important issue is to take the time to decide what is really important to us.
Complex I know but really when we look at how we make our children spend their twelve years of *education*, we could definitely do better.
There is so much energy and desire to do good in each of them but instead we have setup a daycare that is designed to produce good workers for the old system.
It is obvious isn't it, start early and later will be better.
You get out what you put in, blah, blah, blah...

So realistically the main issue is that while the small efforts that we make are all well and good, we are in a race riding a horse against the space shuttle.

Think about it, big business spends every minute of every day meeting and organizing how to maximize profits.

One of the main ways that they do that is by isolating the population and taking away our *free* time.

Oh sure you won't hear that quoted from a CEO.

But once the statistics are analyzed and profits are projected it is just good business to keep us separated in our apart-ments.

We must use the creative potential of our inner knowing and realize that their strength is an illusion.

For example, their propaganda machinery could be used effectively for our benefit and would actually get a stronger return for the love that we put into it.

Another thing to consider is that most of the business *soldiers* are to a large extent working against their will and would be more than eager to be doing something decent for once.

It is only a small minority of the ruling *class* who have nefarious intentions.

Also it may seem that our society is fragmented into a multitude of special interest groups but this isn't by choice.

Their separation is another by-product of the corporate influence and underlying that uniqueness is a strong desire by them to find common ground with all the rest, which would allow all to flourish collectively.

But now the tough pill to swallow, we can't have our cake and eat it too, at least not initially.

Because the majority of the control structures of our civilization were implemented at the mostly behind the scenes request of big business.

And due to the fact that this has been happening for many years, the negative influence is deeply rooted.

Honestly I have looked at the scene from multiple angles.

Occasionally with clarity comes inspiration but the process is gradual.

See the problem, recognize that the situation could be better, and find a way to do it.

"Everything is possible if you wish for it hard enough."

That is where you come in because it is useful to have leaders, heroes, activists, etc.

But individuals are limited in their experience, understanding, and opportunity.

So let's go far reaching and long-term.

And this is where we lose those with short attention-spans.

This isn't a video game with level ups, a television show with heroic triumphs after each hour, or a film with a conclusive ending.

This is long-term and generational but the rewards are there to be sure.

Without wanting to start a religious argument, imagine the change in attitude for North American society if the majority believed in reincarnation or at the very least that we aren't limited to living just this one life.

So many around me are trapped by this one life dogma, accumulating *wealth* for themselves and passing it on to their families as a legacy.

How could racism survive if we all realized that there is a good chance that we were of that ethnicity in the past or will be in the future?

It isn't as simple as if you are the abuser in one life and then you are the victim in the next.

Far more complex and interesting than that.

One way to see it is like we are all threads of the same fabric and if you look close enough at each thread you would see that the pigment changes in numerous places along the way.

So to continue that analogy, let's take that two-dimensional tapestry of humanity and work together to cause us all to fly into the third dimension.

In the same way we can transform our four-dimensional experience into more than any of us can imagine.

If someone were to tell you that they know what *God* has in store for us with any certainty, I would suggest that you run in the other direction.

Take your power back and error on the side of love always.

Now another issue is what many of us feel that we are entitled to or what we deserve.

Of course what gives each of us a functional life is different.

But what works for me is a healthy balance of good food, positive goals, moderate exercise, and *stopping to smell the roses* occasionally.

Which occurs to me is another flaw in our current economic system.

You see, setting prices according to *what the market will bear* will always make the most yearned for things as the most expensive and always just out of reach, like the carrot before the horse.

A great situation for our owners but what are we building?

Some would argue with some merit that while we debate on how to protect ourselves from each other, during the day at work we are helping to strengthen the penal system which is enslaving us.

So in a world where money is power, we must demand transparency and accountability for how our taxes are used.

When we look closely at all the wars of the last century, which is the period of which we have the best understanding, it becomes painfully clear that most were avoidable and usually started to benefit or protect those already in power.

And when we ask for answers and are told that sorry *national security* prevents our being allowed to know the truth, I would suggest that is mostly rubbish.

There are no greater threats to "we the 99%", than those who wield our national agendas like stocks to be bought, sold, and traded.

Also in these discussions there usually arises a rich verses poor argument.

But really what is obvious with only a small investigation is that the only people able to financially afford to seek positions of influence are the ones with a 'vested interest in keeping things as they are.

So yes the poor who take the time to understand their situation soon realize the futility of speaking out as an individual.

And anyone who is oppressed long enough will eventually begin to resent their oppressor whether that controlling force is a person, organization, or country.

Now many of those who have paid attention to *mainstream* history will say that I should stop complaining because things are better now than in *the old days*.

But are they really?

Again the truth will free your mind of this propaganda.

You see, what happens to a large extent is that while we focus on fixing one problem, the compartmentalized *business community* find loopholes to continue maximizing profits.

It usually isn't until people begin to get sick again or a whistle-blower comes forward after their conscience nags them long enough that we find another *cause* to rally behind.

So instead of focusing on single issues (or symptoms), if we want to gain some ground then we need to explore ways of changing the system which allowed or even caused them to happen (the disease).

Once again everyone has their own take on what is important and we need to engage in meaningful discussions on a large scale.

And I would suggest that outside-of-the-box thinking needs to be encouraged as this has been our saving grace numerous times in the past.

I don't have all the answers but I do have faith in our humanity.

Sounds naive I know, but when a person truly investigates the global situation and takes the time to get past the horror and knee-jerk reactions, eventually with desire it becomes apparent that most of these negative situations are significantly influenced by their environment whether it be economic, political, etc.

A long discussion normally ensues now where all the monsters of the past are named, Stalin, Manson, Jim Jones, etc.

But if the environments that those individuals decimated were more stable to begin with then their impact would have certainly been less and they themselves might not have gone to such extremes.

Just a suggestion here but maybe we should find ways to reduce the potential excuses for conflict.

Finally the choice is yours, educate yourselves, empower yourselves, and free us all...

The Now

Okay are we here now, are they there now?

Is it us and them, our 99 verses their 1?

Has the conflict been primed for the revolution?

And do the majority of us really have any clue what is going on?

I seriously doubt it.

Let's CSI this situation.

First thing, has a crime been committed against humanity? Check.

Are we still being enslaved? Check.

Have things actually gotten worse lately? Check.

So let's consider a really important issue.

If there really is a ruling elite who have been running the planet for a long time, does the fact that we can openly discuss revolution mean that the common people are gaining ground?

I would say at this point, not so fast.

You see what I have discovered is that while most people agree that things are bad, nobody can agree on who's to blame or what's to be done.

And when you consider that the majority of the people who are being blamed are themselves just as trapped as most of us, that in itself should give us pause.

Once again I point out that the most important thing that we should be working toward is a loving unified transparent humanity.

So I guess what seems reasonable is to find the changes which do the most good for the least bad and try not to get bogged down in the details.

Another word of warning is to be wary of politicians with 5 or 10 year plans.

It's really easy for them to make promises when the results won't be seen until after they are out of office.

Our plans should be enacted as soon as is safely possible and verified promptly and often.

So many choices, I know.

Like a tightrope walker in the circus big top, we must guide humanity from one safe support pillar to the next without falling away into tangents and distractions.

Also let's not forget about those who are paid *economic hitmen*, agent provocateurs, and of course the flat-out liars.

You see we are quite vulnerable just after we arrive upon a course of action. Like a sports team who has just scored, we must not *rest on our laurels*.

What if we simply ignored the power and influence of those which the majority of us determined to be of negative intentions?

And instead relieved them of their positions and replace them with the vision of our own self-determination, whatever that manifestation becomes. It's easy to bitch and moan about how hard our lives are or to sell-out and turn a blind eye to the suffering of others.

The hard part is to create something new which is worthy of building upon. And rather than starting with a solid foundation which is built upon with weaker material, let's shoot for infinite foundation.

"Intention's the thing, wherein we'll catch the king."

Now politicians, preachers, and revolutionaries will try to mobilize the people by telling us that our country, religion, or cause is better than our enemies.

Obviously I will try my own methods to persuade you of my perspective. I suppose what I am after is not a war but rather a global intervention. Some of our world family need a little tough love but make no mistake it will be love that will heal.

One major flaw with past *revolutions* is that, like a circle, once the overthrow is complete generally not much changes except the people in power.

The few are still dictating to the many whether their tactics be economic, political, religious, ethnic, scientific, etc.

Yes I said scientific.

One issue that I have been keeping an eye on is that science has been growing exponentially while the safeguards to protect humanity, not to mention the planet, from its abuse are few and ineffective.

And the deluge of propaganda continues to desensitize the majority into accepting a situation which is getting worse but which we are told is the way things have always been or, if possible, that things are getting better.

"I never said that it would be easy, I only offered you the truth."

The Matrix films have some good points to make but Hollywood has a way of manipulating the truth not only for profit, but also to rewrite our history and present reality.

The most successful lies contain 90% truth.

Now another important obstacle towards gaining the support from more of the 99%.

Every person on the planet yearns for their own personal form of comfort, which is the most common thing which *the system* caters to.

Whether it be the comfort of home, the acceptance of friends and strangers, or the potent yearning which a parent has to see their children safe.

The idea of losing any of these comforts is strongly resisted, which is why the *causes* which appeal to nearly instant gratification like the quick overthrow of a foreign dictator are so easily embraced.

While anyone who attempts a change here at home must be careful not to put any of those popular comforts at risk, even if it would only be a minor and short-term inconvenience.

Like a student putting themselves through college by working a night job, we need to prioritize in the short-term for a significant long-term goal.

One big point which is important to recognize is that a positive outcome is totally doable.

Here's an interesting thought which should give the detractors ammunition for my firing squad.

If there are more than four dimensions and there are *others* overseeing our planet but with a *prime directive* like in Star Trek...

And if the ancient stories of civilizations being ended in the past for different reasons like Gilgamesh, Atlantis, or Babel are even partly true...

Then my question for our current situation is this...

Would our planetary civilization really be allowed to continue this long if there wasn't the possibility of a positive outcome in our future?

And once I came to that logical conclusion, well then, there's no turning back now kids.

"Scotty, I need warp speed soon!"

So I am creating my better future every day.

Sure there are obstacles, old behaviours, and reflex actions which need to be overcome, avoided, and replaced by something better.

But the most important lesson that I have learned is that I should get past being selfish.

When faced with a solution to a problem that benefits me the most, I must search further for something more.

You see, I know enough to know that I don't consciously have all the answers.

But if I help others and they in turn help more people, then golly the world is round and sooner or later some nice person will eventually find a solution to a problem which I had been struggling with.

Big picture thinking is what we need to teach in schools.

So here's another catch 22 situation.

There is knowledge being withheld for our safety.

No I'm not talking about national security issues or the royal's dirty laundry.

This info that the public is being protected from is the stuff that would cause widespread panics, etc.

We need to prove that we are ready to join the galaxy without being a threat to both ourselves and others.

That's the big picture and we need to get everyone on board peacefully.

Seems like we have a long way to go but I really think that what we need to shoot for is a tipping point when the majority of the population doesn't have a good reason not to join in.

This is starting to sound like a religious teacher sending out missionaries.

And of course all through history there were people with vision who were ridiculed, abused, etc.

I think the difference in this situation is that ever since the first atomic bomb was detonated, we have become the focus of a great deal of attention by the galactic community.

Whereas before that we were left mostly to make our own choices and learn from our mistakes without much interference.

But the stakes are higher now because whether we realize it or not we are negatively effecting other dimensions and things we don't yet perceive.

Now some will say that what I'm proposing sounds a lot like communism and others will take some sound bites out of context and try to make me sound like some past dictator with a negative record.

In all those situations I would simply ask that you not take the *shortcut from thinking*.

By understanding more than the propaganda, dogma, or emotional rhetoric we have a better chance of making a humane decision.

And please don't let anyone convince you that *human nature* is inherently violent, evil, etc.

All the so-called primitive natives who were *discovered* by those with civilization were in fact peaceful and environmental.

Once again I'm not saying that civilization is a bad concept.

However most of us, upon close examination, will agree that we need better and more effective checks and balances at the very least.

So getting back to the detractors, I usually ask them to here me out fully and then discuss any issues that they have.

What I have discovered in all those situations is that usually their negativity stems either from a misunderstanding or because something in my terminology reminds them of a bad past experience.

And actually those are the ones who are able to help me see an issue from a different perspective.

I love you all, peace.

Head Banging

Sometimes I get tired of banging my head against the brick wall of ignorance.
But it never lasts very long, after all I still see the flickers of humanity all around.
And ignorance doesn't bother me as much as the blatant lies of propaganda.
The one thing which occurs to me is that the surveys and questionnaires have convinced the executives that we are all idiots.
I suppose like all empires they have begun to believe their own lies.
And they don't realize that only idiots supply their masters with info which could be used against them.
Also, there will never be a technology which can replace us.
However that hasn't stopped *them* from trying to convince *us* that we are nothing but worker mammals born with *original sin*, etc.
Bullshit!
I have tried many lifestyle variations in this life alone and I have always found my way back to love.
That is just one of the reasons why I believe the default behaviour for humanity is peace, love, and harmony.
Of course that is one of those sound bytes which gets used alone without any background info to make the speaker seem naive or disconnected from reality.
Television at its finest, not!
Another reoccurring theme for me is that it isn't enough to raise the issues and support a cause or two.
That amounts to armchair quarterbacking.
I need to get more involved with the boots on the ground, so to speak.
So let's review, shall we?

Hmm, well I see deficits in our civilization and I have some ideas of how I would like things to be.

I have had discussions with many people of diverse *standing* in this society. All of them agree with most of my points on the issues discussed but they usually lose interest and finish their half of the dialogue with, "Yes, I agree with you but there's nothing I can do about it."

It's hard to argue with that.

So many large protests have gone nowhere in recent years.

Look at the millions who protested against the war in Iraq and Afghanistan. No effect, we still went to war.

Or how about the Occupy Wall Streeters?

Sure they received some support from the main street public but nothing has changed in the checks and balances which allowed the financial collapse to happen in the first place.

Then when it is beneficial for the corporatocracy, all that's needed is a few dozen people wearing similar coloured clothes protesting in a foreign country for us to impose sanctions and put the armed forces on standby.

So like victims of abuse we've learned not to fight back.

After all it's probably our fault anyway, right?

That's a common response with many variations.

One group blames another and like a stubborn child refuses to listen to reason.

And this pattern continues in circles through the years.

One group is right today and another tomorrow.

So long as we are fighting amongst ourselves, we'll never finish building a ladder out of the hole we're in.

Oops, sorry about that.

We've become accustomed to the wild fictions of paperbacks and cinema, so long as it doesn't portray reality too closely.

There is another term for the *yarn I'm spinning*, a conspiracy *theory*.

I heard once that someone was proposing that people should be taxed for discussing *conspiracies*.

Just another example of using economics as a weapon.

But really all I have been doing since I was young is trying to learn the truth.

Sure, no one is perfect and I have believed lies and propaganda in the past.

I will even concede that some of what I believe today may be incorrect but goddamn it at least I'm willing to risk wading into the oceans of information to find the pearls of wisdom.

Occasionally I find something which I think is important and I share it.

The three most common reactions are to say "Wow that's deep.", criticize the format without discussing the message, or the most common of all is complete silence.

WTF?!

As Roger Waters would say, it appears "this species has amused itself to death."

Instead of going to churches, synagogues, temples, etc to learn how much better we are than those who don't attend, maybe we should all get into the habit of getting together and learning how similar we all are and get input from everyone about how to improve our present and future.

No, I'm not saying that our spiritual lives aren't important.

What I'm saying is that most of us are so busy every day that we need to put a priority on fixing the major issues plaguing us daily with the little free time we do have.

As far as spirituality goes, I believe that we all have souls which originated from a common source.

So please, let's stop acting like any one of us is better than another!

And let's stop ripping each other off as a way to survive, just because it seems easier than improving our present environment.

Okay then, back to thinking globally and acting locally.

Two major obstacles to overcome being first, that forward thinking people are rarely listened to in their hometown.

And second, in a situation like the one of our global enslavement, while I focus on helping a few individuals the propaganda and control structures enslave more and more multitudes every day.

Which is why I keep talking about getting more people involved around the globe.

This isn't a Hollywood film where a lone superhero saves us.

We have to save ourselves sooner rather than later.

And that's why I encourage people to truly educate themselves about the reality of our enslavement.

Because the compartmentalized control structures will take effort to dismantle.

Now if I was starting a religion or cult then I would try to convince the followers of my divinity and play on their fears and guilt in order to manipulate them.

But like I have said before the situation is generational and multidimensional.

So if you don't feel called to help this time around, then maybe next time.

The environment has been described with watercolours and the goals have been outlined with pencil, now it is up to us...

Talk about choose your own adventure, sure beats the hell out of cable TV.

And this past season was rigged so I'm pulling my team out of the league (of nations).

"We defeat their authority by ignoring it."

Obviously this isn't for the faint of heart or weekend warriors.

"Never get out of the boat, unless you're prepared to go all the way."

Like eating vegetables when we're young, we need to force ourselves to do the heavy lifting until we get into shape.

"Expecting it to be hard has prepared us for it to now seem normal."

We have tried asking for scraps from the master's table only to be spit upon and laughed at.

And to fight back is beneath us.

Oh sure the propaganda would try to persuade us that we must *fight for our freedom*.

I must admit that fear and anger are potent catalysts, so instead of *reacting*, take the time to *act* in everyone's best interest.

Push past the fight or flight initial impulses.

"If you have to resort to violence, you've already lost."

Let's reinvent what it means to be us.

I won't label us as *people* or *humans* because we all know at our cores that we are far more than that.

And I would suggest that once you get to the point where peace, love, and harmony are some of the strongest desires for you that you then allow yourself to discover the full magnitude of who you/we are.

"Down with the barriers, that we all may be bearers of freedom."

Instead of identifying with your skin or sex, try wearing your inside on the outside.

Let love be your umbrella and a smile be your clothing.

Let your friends be the strangers in the street.

Instead of voting to choose between two similar politicians, why not focus on choosing whether foods, medicines, and technology are safe for us before they are widely distributed?

Like an Etch-A-Sketch, eventually when things get too congested we must turn it upside-down, shake, and start over.

Some believe that Earth is a school for us to learn lessons.

I agree and would suggest that it might be time to upgrade from a high school to a university.

My friends urge me to be patient and I am trying.

I do see many of them catching this celestial wave and hanging twenty, if only the percentages were higher.

An annoying habit leftover from programming 'puters but I am learning to see the big picture more all the time.

A great experience for me isn't zoning out on video games, it's when I'm in the moment connected to the love which holds everything together.

Like right now.

Catching Bees

Health, love, belonging.

Relevant ideas for us all.

But more than that they are the foundation of this enterprise.

When I look around at my friends and strangers, I become aware of those with their insecurities.

Those who overcompensate for the things which they believe they lack.

Those who are overprotective of the things which they are afraid of losing.

Normal human conditions?

Maybe, definitely abundant.

On the rise are the new generation of the isolated.

Those who only interact with other people in person when they have to.

Mostly their insecurities have caused mass isolation where they stay safe behind their email/text screens.

Alone in the crowd with everyone keeping their distance while staring at their phones.

It may seem sometimes like I only have negative things to say but I'm not gonna waste our time by only telling you what you want to hear.

If you want to keep smiling until it makes you sick then take your meds and go to your 9 to 5, have a couple drinks or tokes after you put the kids to bed, sleep and repeat.

Don't worry you'll likely die of an illness long before your ignorant bliss is shattered.

However I will point out to those of you still reading that we are responsible for the environment that we raise our kids in.

The days have long passed when we could say that we didn't have an informed choice.

And how about the poisonous atmosphere that we have helped to create, whether it be physical, spiritual, emotional, etc?

Wouldn't it feel better to know that we are at least trying to improve the situation?

And I'm not talking about voting for *change* every few years.

How about learning what is truly healthy and providing that as a stable environment.

Then with the extra energy and time, we could help to ease the burden on others and ourselves.

I refuse to let any negative emotions have a strong or lasting impact.

I'm building the future with a series of positive presents.

And what makes me smile are the others who show us positive alternatives.

It would appear that much of the current *same old same old* is a product of mass entertainment/propaganda/advertising.

They bombard the senses and leave little time for original thought and creativity.

We either embrace this new environment and become dumbed-down sheeple or we rebel into temporarily isolated outcasts.

But what if the rebels became the majority?

Could we really change things peacefully?

I believe that we can and I believe that our masters are afraid we might succeed.

Don't you ever wonder why every futuristic Hollywood sci-fi movie is a distopian wasteland?

If we continue to believe that there's no way out then we'll continue to take their intoxicants and be satisfied with the occasional happy moment.

What if we invert the situation so the only pain and suffering were the naturally occurring kind?

Impossible you say?!

Nay, I must reply.

But humans have always been warlike you say?!

Don't you ever wonder why so much history is suppressed?

Oh sure we've all done things we'd rather forget and sure the truth hurts sometimes.

But lies are never positive.

Not even the lies told to children, even these should be halted.

Kids seem to be more capable each year and sheltering them is what keeps them from growing.

I am personally curious what groups of young people will produce if they are given the truth and an opportunity to contribute.

And how will the adults act when they can't hide behind parental *national security*?

What if the answers "you're too young to understand" or "you'll understand when you're older" weren't used to avoid revealing an embarrassing truth?

When a person really takes the time to investigate the *established* institutions that most of us can't imagine living without, they eventually realize that those institutions (political, medical, industrial, military) are what is really holding us back.

I know that some of you have remarked that I keep raising similar topics.

And I suppose the reason for that is because I'm hoping to expand on these issues and eventually motivate some of you into positive action, whatever you decide to manifest.

You see what I really love most in this universe is originality, creativity, love, harmony, peace, light, truth, life, etc.

All the things which allow us to feel close together while living our individual lives.

The goal of humanity could be a global love affair with complete respect.

So some say we have to set the example for others to follow and that may be true for some of the issues which are achievable for some individuals to show others.

But really some of the necessary changes are so radical that they require a series of positive moves like a chess match.

And it is hard to *win the game* if you give your opponent advance knowledge of your moves.

Which is why I have alluded to the multidimensional aspect of this journey because if we are in harmony and synchronicity with our *true* path, that makes our actions hard to *predict* and *defend against*.

Now some of these terms sound like warfare or something similar but war requires at least two adversaries and really what we are trying to change is ourselves.

And that is perhaps the most complicated part of this struggle because we all have unique challenges for change.

So if the universe is created and held together with love then I suggest that would be a good place to start for each of us.

Start with love as a foundation and you will be amazed at what you can build.

Frankly I would love to be amazed again.

So much of what is called original these days is simply old building blocks rearranged.

Come on people, you're not trying hard enough!

If you're breathing, you've got an opportunity.

I've got some good ideas for me to do, just you wait...

My future is a blank canvass and I've got watercolours, oils, sparkles, plaster, and invisible ink for starters.

Some people are still clinging to the old propaganda control structures like twelve year long school sentences, weekly religious indoctrination, and the voluntary drugging of those who question the big picture.

Again I point out our potential to combine the best of all loving thoughts like reducing the forced labour of the *lower class* by automating the majority of those jobs with safely redundant machines.

Can't you see that we are being kept busy, tired, and distracted so that we don't revolt in a large organized fashion?

Just look at the justification of income tax while at the same time overspending that money on wars and *black* projects.

And the politicians that we grow to hate are simply cannon fodder puppets for the real powers.

So when someone eventually attempts to assassinate one of them, then those pulling the strings learn to be a bit trickier next time.

Which is how institutions protect themselves and grow.

Okay that was a fun thought exercise but we should probably go back to sleep now.

I mean what's the point of entertaining a possible reality if we don't have the courage to follow through?

Certainly we should provide the basics for health and sanity.

But the rest is there for us to play with.

"Are we having fun yet?"

If we work hard at breaking the negative cycles, then imagine what we could achieve.

Think of all the time and resources expended on dealing with negative situations.

Another helpful point is to provide a true record of reality, be it past or present.

Is it possible to establish a group of independent unbiased caretakers who could help us achieve some of these positive goals?

I truly believe that there are plenty of people qualified but how to get them established in these positions?

We should be able to learn from the past mistakes with many totalitarian dictatorships.

I mean all the empires of the past had great sales pitches.

If only we could turn their lies into the reality of a peaceful, loving, global future.

And resist the tendency for certain pockets of power towards corruption.

A recent study has shown that children begin their lives unselfish.

So if we can help the adults to find their way back to this idea and at the same time provide an environment to assist the kids in maintaining who they truly are.

Peace, love, and harmony achieved through respect, truth, and healthy living.

Good ideas giving birth to other good ideas.

Think about it...

Flip A Coin

Flip a coin, wish on a star, make a choice!

Don't just take it as it comes, go after it with good intentions.

You'd be amazed, fill in the blank.

Be informed, be insane, be interested.

Its not a choice of this or that but of what more to include.

Wikileaks, NSA, Bitcoin, CIA, Pirate Bay, CSIS, Facebook, Corporate Extremists.

You and me, we don't have to leave any thing or person behind ever.

The old formulas have been proven lacking.

Progress, progress, regress.

Two steps forward and one step back.

Like a dance we learned in school, our societies momentum is guided like a roller-coaster.

Is there any proof that the shepherding by the powers-that-be is leading us toward a better future?

Now I'm not saying its all bleak, so let's jump in the abyss.

And I'm also not saying that you should do what I would do or do what I say.

What I'm imploring all humanity to do, both young and old, is become truly informed and actively involved.

So I get asked by the small percentage with a moment of clarity, "Eric, what books should I read? Who should I listen to? What is your ideal future?"

And of course there are those who question, "What the fuck is wrong with you? Who the hell do you think you are? *and* Will you please stop bothering me?"

All perfectly valid questions to be sure.

Write your own book.

Truly listen to the words coming out of your own mouth.

And all I know is that I want you all in my ideal future.

Five

Friends, fiends, winners, losers, famous, infamous.
Happy accidents, planned obsolescence, ignorant bliss.
Going the extra mile, taking an inch, lost in the structure.
Follow the drumming of your heart, but who sets the beat, and who beats the spread?
Could it be you?
Could you be one of the few?
Is there at least two?
Remember why, remember X, remember to get enough sleep.
Pay your way, plan your stay, but do it before you go grey.
In this exponential age time flies by as fast as the speed of light.
Try to anchor your reality onto something meaningful.
Insanity could mean going inside long enough to ponder the truth of the matter and soul.
So put time on hold during the tangents.
Jump start your personal revelation.
How then can we leave the rules behind while bringing forth the peaceful revolution?
We are taught to visualize what we want.
But what we are really looking for is more of a feeling.
Remember that feeling?
You know, the one we all yearn for through the pain.
Home.
As close as we can come to recreating the infinite unconditional love that we came from.
Before time waltzed us through till now.
Be five, see time, look it in the eyes and smile.
Be entirely yourself for starters.

You are the canvass, the billboard, the megaphone, the silent companion,
the observation deck, the muscle car...
How would you feel if someone threw paint on your canvass?
Took down your billboard?
Removed the batteries from your megaphone?
Shattered your silence?
Turned your observation deck into a parkade?
Or laughed while they sped away in your car?
Sure doesn't feel like home to me.
No wonder pharmaceuticals are flying off the shelves.
Neighbourhood bars are packed while our troops fight thousands of miles
away.
And local drug dealers empathize to maximize profits.
Everyone feels it to some extent and cope in different ways.
Some tread water, waiting.
Some head for shore.
Some adapt to a life at sea.
I have made friends with the dolphins.
Humanity thinks, nature winks.
What's beyond the next door?
Is it home?
Is home something I can find or something I have to create?
Can I find or create it by myself?
Or is it something I search for or build with her?
Is she ready?
Am I?
Is it time?
Hold on, I'll ask...

Listening

Holding on too tight.

It leads to more of the same.

Fuckin' jump already!

What you fear couldn't possibly be worse than the reality of your present situation.

Don your armour, grab your weapon of choice, strap on your parachute, and jump.

But before you do, make sure you're in your *right* mind.

Or what's left of your heart, whatever is you the most.

No more fitting in or bending to accommodate the haters, users, and scammers.

Oh shit I forgot that I had made plans to, fill in the blank.

Well I gotta say I live in Vancouver.

And if I postponed my plans on account of the weather, I would still be waiting.

All of us have to jump sometime.

Why else do you think bucket lists are so popular?

Those are the ones who rode the same train their whole lives, or at least the same method of transport.

With so many crucial choices and changes facing us as a society, your informed consent is imperative.

And multiple perspectives are necessary.

I mean, can you see what's behind that billboard or could you hear the visionary next door while you were listening to the radio?

A society of excuses.

Some are futilely trying, or too tired, or have succeeded at a small issue alone, etc.

I'm pulling out all the stops.

Full speed ahead into the sun!

No worries, I'll be back.

But now for my *left* mind.

You know those thoughts which intrude and hold me back from my courageous ambition, to be left behind.

To be always torn in half by the impending future and the fleeting past.

Or is this always but a persuasive illusion?

Like a story about someone telling a story about someone else telling a story...

A natural recursive train of thought.

Someone pull the emergency cord and help me *emerge*.

I will bring with me those truths and revelations.

But not to barter with as that will only distort and dilute.

Hold on, time for the brake.

Like a Matrix moment this time line slows as the scene aligns with the next intuitive path.

Intention's the key, telescope, and beacon of light.

Letting the little one, that little piece of the one, feel its way and point the direction.

Then to take that first step...

Look Both Ways

So I look both ways.
Okay the coast is clear.
My objective is clear.
My mind is clear, crystal.
But don't ask me where we're going.
If you like my intentions, you're welcome to join in.
I'm just a hair on the head of the body trying to gather together the rest of the matter.
Back in the day when I was more naive, some of those trapped in their shadow lives would ask me where I got my views from.
So thinking that they were looking for a little truth to help bring them closer to the light, I was forthcoming with many of my influences.
But of course I omitted divulging the sources of some personal info to protect those sources.
Looking back now I see their selfish motives.
Some wanted to incorporate the info into their masks.
Some needed to find ways of discrediting the sources as though that would make the truth any less valid.
Only a small few were looking for new insights or a secondary confirmation of something they had heard elsewhere.

Like a tightrope walker in the circus big top, long and narrow were the paths between those islands of temporary safety.

But the journey was beneficial in so many ways.

I'm sure Sun Tzu would agree that you can learn a lot about your adversary by what they choose to lie about.

And Rage Against The Machine had a great song called *Know Your Enemy*.

I suppose I thought there were more out there like myself.

I guess my adversaries couldn't imagine that I wouldn't give up.

In the long run our exposure to each other changed us both.

So back to our present, this gift of now.

Let's move forward like a bowling ball.

Staying out of the gutters of negative influence.

It's not about a perfect game but rather steady improvement.

Follow those smiles on the inside, you know the ones.

Those goosebump moments of rightness.

If you can be honest with a child about your day, you're on the right track.

I know, I know, I'm being naive again right?

But honestly, what from the shadows do you really need to hold onto?

Wake up!

Calm Down

Calm down.
Like that statement ever helps.
Somehow we'll make it work.
The kids come first of course.
Then we'll work on you and me.
Rinse and repeat.
Big picture, little snapshot, and the blurry low lit wtf!
Soahc and chaos, look at it forward and back, or close your eyes.
It's up to you, I'll wait.
Take your time, take my time, and I'll buy more.
Hell, I'll steal it if I have to.
Sure don't have to go far to find someone wasting it.
You don't know what you want, right now is emotional overload.
No worries it happens.
What am *I* doing?
Fuckin' breathing in and out!
That's enough for now.
I could be walking down the road with my water wings, 'cuz you never know.
But you're always on my heart and it still beats a little faster every time I think about us.

There's no point to any of it, just that one feeling.

You know the one.

The one I start the day with when I roll over and see you next to me.

Those days are limitless.

I can bend time to my will.

No longer just trying to make you smile, I'm writing a screenplay every day.

All about us and us above all but it's all relative.

Shit, I haven't kissed you in forever, nearly an hour.

My last chance, the fear is paralyzing sometimes.

Never want this dance to end, even when the music stops and we just stand there together, the rest of the world dances around us.

The constant embrace, even when we're apart.

Our children are learning the most important thing.

What love looks like, feels like, and needs to grow.

It has taken root for us in the ether.

That invisible everywhere which shelters us always.

We is this, you are me, I am our kids.

Energy flowing around and through us in a closed loop.

Morphing, creating, and disappearing, only to return as something we couldn't have found individually.

Wow, I gotta get some sleep sometime...

There There

Haters gotta hate, not.

They should check themselves before they say or do anything.

There is a saying I read in the Bible, "It's not what you put in your mouth that contaminates you but rather what comes out."

And of course my mom taught me not to say anything unless I had something good to say.

But I amended that to allow for constructive criticism.

Of course we should cover our basics.

Yup, food clothing shelter.

But closely following those foundations could be the generous intentions towards our immediate family and friends.

Once again I will point out that a person alone will only achieve a fraction in comparison to the exponential growth of human cooperation.

So build from the good stuff imagined from within.

Deprogram yourself from the propaganda dreams sent to you in those oh so pretty packages.

Like the daily struggle not to become more like the rulers from the old world, in this life nothing really worthwhile is easy.

At times the hard part for me has been to find some quiet lucid moments to regroup and choose my next pursuit.

Do you have some noble goals inside you that you don't share?

That is another of those necessary foundations but one which is seldom talked about.

Lately we tend to spend a lot of time just maintaining what we've got.

The silly thing is that, from another perspective, what we thought was important can now be seen as rather trivial.

In many respects life is a school filled with moments of experience.

If you could take a snapshot of this moment, would it make it into the photo album?

Is it something you could share completely later?

How much of our time do we spend rationalizing why it's okay to do this or that?

For that matter, do we often rationalize not asking ourselves questions like that in the first place?

Hell maybe I should just fill the page with question marks and in the centre just put, "Do you know who you are?"

Try everything or at least visualize whatever interests you.

Do you understand yourself?

How can I understand you if you can't even be honest on the inside?

Barriers within barriers.

Illusions being bounced off mirrors and projected onto the walls.

It could be fun, depending on the subject matter.

And with our leaders' motives even more cryptic than our own, we certainly have a hard time going along with the big show.

So back to the conflict raging perpetually onward.

It certainly is easier to hate than to love for any prolonged period.

What the fuck, I give up!

Ya right, not bloody likely!

Maintain all of it all at once, why not?

What else are you gonna do?

But don't answer that out loud, keep your main true intentions inside but not forgotten.

Or maybe not, of course you have to decide what is best for you and yours.

Apparently the big idea which I keep coming back to is to get a more informed understanding of the big picture from your perspective.

Apathy is no longer a socially acceptable default setting.

As the saying goes, "Shit or get off the pot!"

Our lives are gifts that we are privileged to experience.

If you can't see that basic understanding, Google ignorance and look in the mirror.

Okay the rest of you, one thing that has become more apparent every day is that with privilege comes responsibility.

Pretty self-evident to me.

But also a term which has been distorted in naziesque fashion.

The responsibility of the privileged is to protect themselves and their friends... Not!

Or when that appeal doesn't work, let's try showing them that the odds of really affecting a positive change are slim at best.

Nope, still bent on doing some good, hey?

All right but you'll be doing it all alone.

Your friends won't understand you know?

There now you're listening.

Okay back to doing your part in the big lie...

Censorship Masterpiece

War!

Be war e!

I had to walk out of a movie theatre halfway through the film.

In my life, I have seen some progress towards equality, etc.

But when it comes to the enemies or potential enemies of our country and its allies...

Well shit, the propaganda and ridicule used to dehumanize those targets is embarrassing for me.

There are two major reasons that have kept me from travelling outside of Canada in my adulthood.

The first is that I have never made any attempt to hide my political, religious, or any other views.

The second is due to our country being drawn into so much *peace keeping*.

Anyway, back to the next war.

It seems pretty obvious that we are being conditioned to accept a war with China and its *allies*.

But don't worry, it's not like you are gonna have to struggle with a *yay* or *nay* vote.

Your quiet obedience is all that is required.

And make sure to invest your portfolio in weapons manufacturers and *re* construction firms.

If the spin doctors do their jobs well, you'll be cheering on the best damn video coverage ever!

No worries, with their internet firewall, we'll only see the images approved of by the high command.

Spoiler alert, to quote George Orwell (Eric Blair) from the novel 1984, "2+2=5 and Oceania has always been at war with Eurasia."

But all that is above your pay grade, right?

Or how about *that could never happen without a good reason.*

If you read a book or watch a lecture by Noam Chomsky, it will become obvious how the media can be used to *Manufacture Consent*.

Oh well another blood stain on the wall from repeated blows by my head.

Just another day hoping for the best and planning for the worst.

Nazi concentration camps have set the benchmark for what truth seekers have to endure.

No I'm not asking for sympathy or claiming to be a hero or the like.

Just a friendly reminder to the adversary, we are prepared for whatever your selfish greedy little fingers get up to next.

Do you ever wonder why the bully hates the nerd?

It's because the bully knows what he is doing is wrong, but denies it.

While the nerd tries to find a solution to the argument and teach the bully.

But the bully fears changing because that is the only life he has ever known.

So it's easier for him to persecute the nerd.

Another impediment to the bullies taking over the planet is the spiritual guidance which has helped time and again to get humanity back on track.

But really it's not a matter of us protecting ourselves from them or even correcting their mistakes.

We need to deny them the approval for their wrongdoing in all its forms.

Like children in the sandbox, their behaviour will change until they get what they really need.

So long as the Machiavellian masters continue to reign over this monetary prison we will continue to bear witness to chaos without perceptible rhyme or reason.

And so long as the historical record remains a censorship masterpiece, we will remain content in this as a perceived normality.

Okay, deep breath.

Like basic training, all standard beliefs and behaviours are gone now.

So let's build us up in proper fashion to become better versions of ourselves.

And from within our solid foundation, we will project a more stable environment.

Let's be the creators that we were always capable of.

Instead of spending our down time paying for ways to escape the drudgery of the day to day, we could instead build a better unreality.

Okay we will now open the floor to questions...

Musical Chairs

Rain begins its onslaught once again.

But I don't mourn at its arrival today.

In fact from my perspective I imagine the saturation of those exposed like lost souls enlightened by the everlasting light of creation.

All responding in different ways to its influence.

Some run for cover and try to shake it off, like a kitten recently disciplined with a squirt bottle.

Some try to protect themselves physically with umbrellas, coats, and hats.

They tiptoe quickly between the puddles with sad eyes, like exiled prisoners.

My favourites are those who stand in dry protection momentarily, before making the brave decision to surge out into the chaos.

They are quite exposed out there, while making every effort to shield their phones like a mother for her child.

So what of the lasting effects of this brief spiritual shower?

Does it cost more to invest in protection rather than adapt, accept, or even try to understand?

I learned a long time ago that if I want someone to read a certain book, handing it to them and suggesting that they read it is not a very successful strategy.

Instead I was instructed to set a good example with my own behaviour and drop an odd reference to the book in passing while leaving the book laying out in the open for anyone to read.

Indeed that strategy is far more successful.

But I have to ask the obvious question...

Why is subterfuge required to share the truth?

No really I'm asking?

Of course from my perspective there are a number of possible reasons.

But honestly what I am really hoping for is that more truth will be made available and that more reasonable people come forward to affect a positive change.

But there are so many past examples of those trying to do the *right* thing being shot or at the very least ridiculed into silence.

Few and far between are those with both the courage and the understanding to make a positive change.

There are numerous reasons to stop short of meaningful interaction.

I mean Edward Snowden had to hide on the other side of the planet in order to protect himself from a backlash to revealing the truth about his government breaking the law.

And Julian Assange is still hiding in a friendly embassy after more than two years, simply because he helped other whistle-blowers get the truth out.

But even the truths which they revealed are lost in the propaganda storm filled with images of Miley Cyrus, Justin Bieber, and YouTube kittens.

Or how about all those false flag *wars, revolutions, and terrorism* designed to keep our police and armed forces from going after the *real* criminals higher up the food chain?

All the while the surveillance apparatus in our countries takes away more of our privacy every day.

Of course there is the old argument that you shouldn't be concerned if you don't have anything to hide.

But let's be honest with ourselves for a moment (I know, there's that word again).

Honest (*adjective*) – Honourable in principals, intentions, and actions; Upright and fair.

If we take a moment internally to do a thorough inventory of our secrets and questionable past behaviours, most of us will have a fair amount of dirt that we would prefer to keep hidden under the rug.

So the omniscient surveillance makes us all into slaves to the state.

Like minimum wage workers being watched by CCTV.

One false step or straying off the work quota is punishable.

No wonder we are constantly stabbing each other in the back.

Like global fucking musical chairs.

Shit the music just stopped!

Suck It Up

Life long, life short, after life?
Okay I'm alive, so now what?
Can I get a do over?
Would I really want to go through the first half again?
Suck it up soldier!
Like one of those spy films.
You know when the people in the surveillance van try to isolate a certain conversation out of a noisy crowd.
In all the white noise of our civilization, how do I narrow down my true calling?
Or is that just another one of those fictitious Hollywood inventions?
All right let me do my Jack Nicholson impersonation, "What if this is as good as it gets?"
If I ever really believed that, I would have jumped years ago.
Like someone who had true love for a short time before their partner passed away, I am burdened with the knowledge that there is so much more available out there.
And with no significant other or offspring, my choices are wide open.
What would you do?
I have been the good guy, the bad guy, the lost guy, and the found guy.
The voice of reason, the ignorant overconfident voice, the insane voice, and the voice crying out in the wilderness.
I have tried reason, love, lust, humour, humility, humanity, luck, chance, faith, and even politics.
It sure has been a ride to remember all right.
But a mostly solo flight.
Shit, I'm starting to depress even myself.
The nice thing about living in the big city is that there are always distractions available, for a price.
But it's a bit like the image of a guy on an exercise bike powering the television set he's watching.
With thoughts like that it's no wonder I'm still single.
Hold on ladies don't crowd me, one at a time please.
Sure I could be one of those assholes who learn how to make women think that he really cares when in fact it's more of a reality show that he's trying to win.

Divorce rates and the percentage of single parents will attest to that.

Can we ever find a golden age again?

Would it really be much different than now?

Running to stand still, all the best lines have been sold to the money factory.

Oh sure there are a couple dozen films a year made for the Oscars.

But the rest are mostly technicolor Twinkies that provide just enough of a sugar rush to sustain you up until the credits roll.

Then you roll your eyes and try not to think about how you got duped once again.

Remember corporations don't vote against their own interests.

We are like worker ants in an ant hill cult.

Most of us work hard at our subjugation and then hand over the majority of our supposed *income* to purchase things which will distract us from the final *outcome*.

No wonder the 99% are being drugged and hypnotized en masse.

If we were all awake at once, the 1% would be zero percent pretty fast.

No I'm not talking death by crucifixion, guillotine, or hanging.

A non violent overthrow by simply not recognizing the authority of Kings, Queens, Dictators, and Corporations is more like it.

But of course waking up out of our stupor is only the beginning.

Those with organizational gifts need to work on a transitional strategy.

And the dreamers, futurists, and architects can design us something to look forward to.

Really, is there any other choice?

The only other two choices I see are to continue with our present slavery or to rebel sporadically in disorganized anger.

The first choice would obviously lead to more of the same as no king or dictator in history has ever given up power voluntarily.

The second choice is the one they've been preparing for, which gives them excuses for martial laws and genocides.

The later also makes us easier to control with more restrictions and less people.

Of course that's just my perspective.

I am always open to positive input.

But please no self serving arguments raised in the hopes of simply delaying the inevitable.

And certainly no lawyers at all as the process of passing the bar automatically disqualifies you all.

Definitely putting out a call to all amateur freedom fighters looking to go pro.

Another new strategy to ponder is how to get organized in the first place.

Please recognize that Facebook, Gmail, Twitter, and the like are all recorded, archived, and monitored in real time.

All that is needed is one key phrase to be flagged and then that person is focused on and all those who have had contact are then closely scrutinized.

Definitely time to go old school in that respect.

Really when you think about it, it's an unstoppable inevitability.

There are no races anymore, no religions, no sexes, etc.

Just the masters vs the slaves.

Another point to consider is that my friends and I spend a lot of time and energy making the case for a change.

And of course there will be tough times on both sides.

So we need to be very aware of deceptions at the end of the main hostilities.

Remember, you get what you settle for.

Also, along the way we will be tempted to put some people up on pedestals.

But that whole hierarchical structure is a scam used to keep the slaves beholden to a ruler.

Obviously phony national security, black budgets, and a general lack of transparency are situations to avoid.

But the question then becomes what to replace them with.

Like a twelve step program we have taken the first step and admitted that we have a problem, in fact a multitude of them.

But there are no manuals or history books that can guide us through a complete overhaul of the system.

Don't you ever wonder why we have no detailed history of previous civilizations older than four thousand years or so?

It sure would be nice to have a true record of what happened to those who came before us.

Maybe we could learn from their mistakes.

What if that's why we are kept ignorant, like the Bible story about the tower of Babel?

Remember, remember the 5th of November...

Cart Before The Horse

The cart before the horse, the Universe before the Earth, picking out baby names before finding the right partner.

The problems have been isolated, the sides have been drawn, the propaganda relentless...

But do enough good people really give a fuck?!

I mean the distractions, pacifications, disinformations, and flat out ignorances are bloody staggering.

The Tragically Hip have a really good song titled *Ahead By A Century*.

Many of those in power argue that most people aren't ready for true freedom or the power to choose their own destiny.

And to a certain degree I would agree.

To go from the ignorance and slavery of our recent daily experience, then to be truly free and responsible is indeed a large leap.

But the idea in the minds of myself and my friends has always been a nonviolent transition involving education and participation based upon the true history and true understanding of our collective realities.

Of course the grand idea is still fluid and open.

But isn't that better than the perpetual greed, infighting, backstabbing, and rape by every definition that are going on all the time now?

I really don't agree with the idea of constantly creating industries and products to deal with and treat the never-ending symptoms spewed forth from the festering sore that is our out-of-control civilization!

Some say that we should put the women in charge.

And for the most part, with a level playing field, that's not a bad idea.

Kind of like when the Americans vote in a Democrat after growing tired of a Republican.

At the very least they couldn't do any worse than us guys have done.

But really both genders are being manipulated so much that if you were to take a guy and a gal from one of our cities and put them next to a pair from an untouched natural setting, wow.

Just imagine it!

Everybody's got a story about where we went wrong or a group they believe is responsible.

But with everybody pointing a finger and yelling, it turns into white noise TV snow that finally gets unplugged just so we can get some sleep.

What matters is now and what we are willing to do to help.

Recognizing that bandages don't cure cancer, we must dig deep enough to pull out the roots of the most entrenched problems.

Getting past our own greed, bias, prejudice, and all other behaviours which keep us at odds with each other is a crucial first step.

Like the chess master said to the student, "See the whole board."

But don't let emotion cloud your judgment or cause you to act at an ineffective time.

Remember that in every battle there is offence and defence.

Making small gains can be eclipsed by large losses.

One of the most popular forms of pacification that I have noticed in multiple cultures and mediums is the idea that a single hero, group of heroes, deities, magical groups, politicians, and or political parties can somehow save us all.

That certainly makes a nice Hollywood film but the percentages are pretty low in reality.

And unless you have a time machine or a way to cause those in the highest positions of influence to suddenly A) grow and B) follow their consciences, it will take many more of us in our lower positions to first even out the odds.

Then with our heads above water for the first time in millennia, we would have a better perspective to plan a better future.

Small gains are fine so long as those are the results of the efforts.

But usually in order to get those small gains the initial targets need to be much larger.

This is so for reasons including but not limited to the many necessary compromises and the fact that a majority vote requires more than just our own votes.

Like Monsanto grain blowing into a neighbouring field, our small gains can lead to much more.

There is a great line in the song *Hard Road* by the Sam Roberts Band, "It's all right to get caught stealing back what you lost."

Remember, Hitler was able to do most of his nefarious deeds by first altering the morality of his people through propaganda and appealing to various human weaknesses.

This was done systematically by removing the checks and balances to his authority.

So in my own way, one of the underlying themes in all my writings has been to point out that many of these tactics are still in use today.

Not to start another 9/11 debate but just look at how that one day and event has encouraged more racism than any other in recent memory.

History shows that if you want to understand the causes of world changing events, one need only look to who truly benefits.

And I'm not talking about International Banking and Propaganda Inc. aka CBS, NBC, ABC, FOX, etc.

The one advantageous thing about our present situation is that those propagating the negative deeds deem themselves untouchable.

So in reality the same groups and persons can be seen to be involved in multiple acts over numerous years.

And if a person is truly interested in the big picture, well shit, enough people have already connected many of the dots.

But like that crucial moment in the original Matrix film, the hardest choice is in the beginning with whether to take the blue pill or the red pill.

And before you make your decision, realize that being a weekend warrior won't accomplish much.

Like Martin Sheen in Apocalypse Now, once you get out of the boat you must be prepared to go all the way.

Of course what *all the way* means is different for everyone.

And maybe part-time at first could lead to full-time at last.

After all there is a high turnover for this job.

But like I said before, the future is fluid and my perspective is largely speculative.

Now for a warning.

There are those whose job it is to entrap would-be do-gooders.

It's pretty simple really, they agree with what you're passionate about.

And then, of course, they tell you what you want to hear.

Over a prolonged period and after many lies and manipulations, you are backed into a corner or no win scenario.

The end result is that however good and true your intentions were to begin with, you are now twisted, jaded, and compromised.

And if your good works become too much of a threat, you can be easily smeared in the court of public opinion if not actual court.

So that's the sales pitch.

Sounds pretty inviting doesn't it?

However that's not the only opening available.

A secondary assignment is the idea that it is long past time to stay silent in our personal lives.

So when someone behaves in a way which is contrary to the furthering of the good fight, I encourage everyone to challenge that person on where they got those beliefs or ideas.

Personally I'm pretty comfortable in my beliefs as I have been discussing the major issues for many years now.

So, when someone behaves like a racist, for example, I stop just short of a citizen's arrest.

Now a reminder.

In the previous examples, I am talking about personal interactions one on one and in person.

I have discovered that it is pretty useless to chastise someone on Facebook, etc!

What usually happens is that they act polite and even agreeable online and then are anything but behind the scenes where they aren't being recorded or seen by their *friends*.

Like the old IRA ideology about defeating the English occupation by simply ignoring their authority, we can side-step Big Brother by going old school in our really real interactions.

And of course it is important to realize that any meetings of two or more people will be scrutinized.

So it is important to maintain your integrity (i.e. practice what you preach) in all you do.

Play time is over.

For a long time now I have lived as though I was being watched at all times.

To quote Dan Aykroyd from the film Sneakers, "The question is not whether you're paranoid but whether you're paranoid enough!"

Be worthy of the future that you want.

Be aware of the fine print for the things which you desire.

Be healthy in your needs and yearnings.

Be a better version of yourself than the expected versions of the people who you criticize.

Let's call it Plan Be.

Bedtime Story

Alrighty then, I suppose it's time for a lovely comforting bedtime story.
Well let's see if we can read one that you haven't heard before.
Oliver Stone's film JFK is a wonderful production but for the sake of this
story I will recall only one line.
"How do you know who your daddy is? Because your mamma told you so!"
There are so many things that I recognize now as being complete bollocks
even though 9/10ths of those asked would say otherwise.
No I'm not talking about internet advertising or the lies teenagers tell their
parents.
What today's story is about is the very foundational beliefs we are born into
and raised with.
You know, who we are, where we came from, who we should trust, and who
the bad guys or gals are.
Ya I know, that's a pretty broad statement.
So let's narrow it down to one topic because we need to get some sleep
sometime.
Let's get to know the bad guys, shall we?
Starting with World War Two because that was a pivotal point in global
affairs.
Yup the Nazis were assholes all right.
But more truth keeps coming out about the real facts leading up to the
German *expansion* and what the Soviets were doing before Hitler invaded.
Also the antagonism of Japan by the Americans prior to the attack on Pearl
Harbour.
And of course most of us have heard by now about the many banks and
corporations that funded and supported both sides in most of the conflicts.
Not to mention the many families and individuals who have conveniently
forgotten how they happily went along with and even encouraged the
racism, sexism, and many forms of zealotry which allowed certain groups to
round up and/or exterminate various other groups during the war.

Of course the sanitized history claims that Hitler seduced or hypnotized the German people against their will.

And we are told that the Japanese were manipulated by their honour etc.

Or that the poor Russians were just sitting around *not doing nothing* when Hitler attacked them.

As so often happens reality is stranger than fiction.

About the only true facts from the victors history books concerning that period are that a hell of a lot of brave soldiers and innocent civilians were sacrificed for no good reason.

Okay that's enough for WW2.

Next up is to simply mention the name, Vietnam.

So much has been written in books and portrayed in films that it is now abundantly clear what a dirty war that was.

Once again too many soldiers and civilians died in horrific conditions for no good reason.

This time we have a more descriptive name for the bad guys, The Military Industrial Complex.

The assholes running this show have turned our world into a rigged high stakes poker game.

More recently we come to 9/11, Iraq, and Afghanistan.

So much has already been said by others that I will simply point out a few lesser known facts.

The first point I always make is to follow the money.

Is it a huge coincidence that when 9/11 occurred, the U.S. Armed Forces defence budget was due to be cut dramatically.

But due to the attacks on that one day, not only was the budget not cut but it has more than doubled since.

Another interesting point is the validity of the videos of Osama Bin Laden.
Personally I don't speak his language.
So I have no way of knowing what he really said on the many videos shown on the news.
It was claimed by the pro war proponents that he took responsibility for the attacks.
However other translators have said that he never did take responsibility no matter how hard you listen.
And an interesting story was in the news last week, some 13 years later.
A man accused of being a participant in the attacks on 9/11, asked to have a translator removed because he recognized him as having worked at the Guantanamo Bay detention facility.
Talk about rigging the game.
And now we come to the presumably inevitable war on ISIS.
First off to give the mainstream media a sound byte, ISIS sounded backwards sounds like sissy...
But really to get serious, how can anyone really believe that these clowns are anything other than a front to stir up anger in the targeted countries?
Which is another point that I bring up about 9/11.
In terms of long-term strategy, both 9/11 and the ISIS beheadings certainly aren't furthering any positive goals for either of the assumed perpetrators.
It seems to me that there is far more going on behind the scenes.
Hmm, who really profits from constant global conflicts and *apparent* terrorism?

Yada Blah Etc

Hello.

Hello, is this thing on?

Good.

All right then, let's be perfectly clear.

This is NOT a video game.

This is a serious conversation about the world we live in.

This is OUR reality.

In the video games, as long as you have the best score when time runs out, you win.

However in this reality which we all share, time continues beyond your attention span and we inherit tomorrow what we leave today.

The apathy of the majority is what condemns our future.

Sure it is fun and liberating to live in the moment when the only concern is the hangover you'll have in the morning.

Definitely parents need to provide for their kids.

But how did we get to the point where the only ones thinking about long-term planning are dictators, corporations, and *intelligence* agencies?

Was it a certain advertisement that finally convinced you to only care about you and yours?

Because if you watch little kids, they are so unselfish that their elders end up teaching them to "Think before they act."

Etc, blah, blah, blah...

We all know what the right thing is.

But all those *innocent* surveys that we politely answered have given the statisticians of master manipulators all the weapons that they will ever need.

Knowing how much bullshit we'll swallow before turning off the PlayStation.

Like the frog in the pot this water has been boiling for a while now.

And some are digging into their pockets hoping they've got enough to buy a tea bag.

Fuck that!

It's time to human pyramid our way out of this mess.

Come on, use those puzzle solving skills that got you past the last level on your game of choice.

Let's call this a potential distopian reality simulation.

Most of you have been born with a cutting edge pair of high resolution VR goggles. Powered by a cold-fusion multi-core processor and the latest in sensor technology. Yada, yada, yada, you get the point.

Human up already.

In this MMO you can't get more than a level ahead of those in your sphere of influence.

And there is a time bonus for helping to bring others along.

Now of course there will always be the selfish haters who will nit pick every word.

What do I mean by "Bringing others along?"

Sounds kinda cultish, dictatorial, or even pyramid scheme like.

But as I noted earlier what we're talking about is progressively improving our collective sit-u-ation.

For the sake of simplicity, let's consider everyone as being equally deserving of respect.

And what if the only points that you get at the end of the game are for helping others.

Bonus points for unselfish acts of kindness, etc.

You know the drill.

Time for a mental cleanse to flush those toxic Hollywood stereotypes and government/corporation sponsored propagandas.

Of course these ideas will be resisted by those with a moderate to high level of comfort.

You know, the cynical, tired, jaded, abused, etc.

Who for many reasons believe that because they worked hard (in their opinion) and achieved the status that they deserve (again their perspective)...

Well golly if everyone just *smartened up* and followed the rules, yada, blah, etc.

To mix my movie metaphors, "If you build it, they will come."

But if you rely on scaring people into submission then it is only a matter of time before they see behind the curtain.

I seem to remember a few people back in the 60s saying some similar stuff.

The weapons used to resist the suggested ideas then were as varied as they were creative.

Don't get me wrong I truly believe that the vast majority of those in the lower parts of the hierarchical pyramids of the compartmentalized organizations referred to as *The Corporation, The Government,* and *The Company* are well meaning patriotic individuals who are working hard for what they believe to be the right reasons.

But we need to hold those who are higher up (in more ways than one) and giving the orders, accountable.

Now another challenge for you all.

Many of the people who have some insights into what's really going on get so isolated and angry that eventually when they get to the "what's to do" segment, they say how hopeless it all seems, etc.

And when I pin them down to the main reasons for these feelings of despair the most common statement is that everyone else is either lazy, stupid, or just plain ignorant.

Now hold on don't smile, I'm being completely serious.

How can a society work together on the important issues of our time when we don't even really like or trust most of our fellow citizens?

Personally, well most of you know by now where I'm coming from.

The more true info we can all absorb, the better.

Because knowledge is power and in this case it is crucial for the ability to grasp the big picture.

We are all one big global family.

Oh sure some of us are the crazy aunts and uncles.

And some of us just want the peace, quiet, and stability to raise our kids, etc.

Nothing wrong with that.

But with the present state of world affairs, the only way to secure that stability is by constantly keeping the Jackboots on the the throats of any potential threats.

That doesn't really seem like a sustainable situation to me.

But I could be wrong.

Play out the tape on that perspective.

Let's see now, how many violent or dictatorial empires evolved into peaceful utopias.

Nope, I didn't think so.

But if you've got a better idea, I'm all ears, eyes, etc...

Enemy Of The State

Well then, I have decided that there isn't much point in only going halfway insane. The reality of the global drama is so completely polarized.

Let me invoke Revelation 3:16 for this situation.

Here is the NIV translation for those who don't remember it, "So because you are lukewarm – neither hot nor cold – I am about to spit you out of my mouth."

Alrighty then, let's talk about evil shall we?

Yup, I'm cannon balling into the deep end.

What if the idea of evil is valid but the accurate definitions have been suppressed?

What if there is a reason why we as a global community haven't reached a widespread and lasting peace after more than 3000 years of conventional history?

I mean really, I have a pretty good feeling about most of us 99%.

And we all agree that there is good, that there is bad, and that something should be done about it.

So why isn't that the main focus of our newscasts (I know that's an outdated term), books, and films?

Oh sure, we have lots of cartoonish and absurd examples that make money without really saying anything.

Which reminds me of a topic that is guaranteed to piss off most Christians.

In 325 A.D. a group of politicians, clergy, and noblemen voted on what should be included in what we now call the Christian Bible.

Kind of reminds me of the *official* investigation into 9/11.

So let's do a little critical thinking about the New Testament.

If there really was a guy named Jesus who saw the truth about good and evil in his times, does it seem like a positive thing that his messages were only written down more than 50 years after his death?

Or that more than 200 years later, once the movement we now call Christianity had gained a sizable following, the same types of people who Jesus had apparently been critical of then decided which version of his message should be allowed?

Talk about censorship.

From then till now, many similar so-called leaders have threatened, imprisoned, tortured, and killed beyond count anyone who questioned the official *story*.

Sure does sound like an enlightened group alright.

No wonder the royals claim a divine right to rule and those popes obviously had a hot-line to God.

But don't worry I'm not gonna go into detailed definitions of what I believe to be the correct interpretations of the New Testament.

Except to say once again that we all know right from wrong if we care enough to weigh the consequences of our actions.

I remember *back in the day* when I was hangin' with the tough guys, one of them gave me a clarifying ultimatum, "Do you want to be the steamroller or the road?"

Of course I knew what he wanted to here.

But now I realize that I have always been part of the road.

Not only that but I gave the steamroller permission to roll over me time after time.

That seems to be a reoccurring theme, we get tricked into giving our power away.

"The greatest trick the Devil ever pulled was convincing the world he didn't exist."

Once again I could go on and on about my perspective concerning who the Devil is or whether he or she actually exists.

Or the validity of possession and exorcism, or the existence and/or location of hell etc.

But it is a lot like when the cops post a description of some suspected criminal.

If that info finds its way to the suspect then some obvious modifications occur and before long the suspect is back to mingling freely.

Also if you compare the various descriptions of evil down through the years, it seems quite clear that evil is a chameleon changing at will.

So obviously we need a foolproof test.

Okay if you suspect someone of being evil then throw them into deep water and if they float then they are evil but if they drown then they were good.

Sounds pretty logical.

But seriously, my personal experience with evil is varied.

One example which is relevant for now and the future is the drug cartels.

We now live in a culture which not only condones but actually encourages intoxication in various forms.

Consider that you can't get through 30 minutes of prime time television without one of the characters either drinking alcohol or getting high.

Of course there is now a law prohibiting smoking and drinking in commercials.

But the alcohol and tobacco lobbies can throw their money towards period pieces where their products were more socially acceptable.

So once again we have chain-smoking hard drinking protagonists who we are conditioned to empathize with.

And just a general question here but why is it that whenever someone in a Hollywood film has a bad day, fights with their boy/girlfriend, or rebels against their parents or other authority figures, that scene usually leads them to either get drunk or high?

It is as if we are repeatedly told that these are the only natural reactions to these situations.

With all the shit going on in our cities, countries, and planet shouldn't more time be spent showing citizens how to organize in peaceful demonstrations that actually have a positive outcome?

I mean, WTF?!

Does anyone have a logical answer to why less is being done now concerning the factors which are negatively affecting us?

Is it that most have given up the fight?

Or is there a more dire reason for their apathy?

Like, is there so much corruption and *illegal* activity pervading most areas of society that most people's very support systems rely so heavily on these alternative incomes that getting a majority to agree to change is tantamount to a fool's errand?

Shall we all just collectively fiddle while our society physically and metaphorically burns to the ground?

Come on people, it's not like we can't see the signs!

Okay, I would usually leave it at that.

But today I've got to say that the fact that I have to even point this stuff out, really pisses me off!

Either you have been reading this or you are hearing it being read.

Either way, the fact that you are still tuned in at the end is commendable.

However, I have to say at this point that you are likely the only one out of thousands.

Or there is an outside chance that others have been planning and organizing off the grid.

I sure hope so but wishful thinking is only the beginning.

Today's morality challenge, what did you do today to make the world a better place?

Planning 101

Let the planning begin!

First thing, maybe we'll start with an anonymous suggestion box.

Including nominations for lead organizers in various categories, which is not to say positions of power but rather people who are recognized as having both the experience in the necessary fields and are motivated to lead the way towards some positive changes.

There are numerous stories of prisoners of war who maintained their sanity by methodically building things mentally, day after day.

I am quite sure that there are many people today who, though not prisoners in the same sense, feel trapped by an archaic system and have also built things in their minds.

Only these thought projects aren't tractors or the like.

Rather they have inspirations like science fiction, a two hour Hollywood pacifism, or other money making projects which provide just enough hope to fleece the suckers.

These people take a good idea here or expand on an unformed idea there.

They have given a lot of thought to out-of-the-box possibilities to improve our global situation.

So with some of the encryption techniques revealed by Edward Snowden, Julian Assange, and others, we should be able to set up a secure drop box for these and other suggestions.

Which then presents another hurdle.

Somehow we then need to sort through and combine, refine, or expand on viable projects.

By now I am sure that many of you can grasp the points that I am making. It is not really all that original.

Many governments and other organizations employ many of the same processes.

However nothing of this size or flavor has ever been tried before.

Oh sure some people will bring up examples like The United Nations or smaller organizations like Amnesty International, Greenpeace, etc.

They will point out that although many of those groups appeared to have had good intentions, they were ultimately fighting an up hill battle or no win scenario.

So how can we, the little people, hope to achieve better results?

That is on the surface a fair question.

But if you scratch the surface and dig a little deeper, the reasons for their lack of success will become apparent.

Many of these have been issues that I have raised at length previously. Suffice it to say that many of the reasons go to a general lack of transparency and accountability, which ultimately lends itself to a detachment of the generals from the common soldiers resulting in both having differing intentions and goals.

So finally we see our present political and corporate landscape mirroring our own dysfunctional personal lives.

Another common argument made against the possibility of global peace is that *human nature* prevents us from being able to get on the same page enough of the time to form a lasting cessation of hostilities.

Which of course is another of those issues which I have discussed at length previously.

I believe that humanity working for humanities sake can result in many unexpected positive things.

It is when we are forced to do what George Orwell referred to as *double think* which causes most of the tragedies we see daily.

So you get situations like when a father is forced to do things which he hates and/or which hurt others around him so that he can provide for his family who have been put in an extraordinarily bad situation.

You all know the drill.

They say that money is the root of all evil.

But it isn't the dollars, pounds, or yen which are to blame.

But rather the use that people put that money to, which allows them to have unnatural power over others.

Which is where we get the whole legal system from.

It isn't to protect the average person but was instead created to discourage us from fighting back against the establishment by imposing set punishments for *unruly* behaviour.

Anyway back to Utopia.

If you even mention the term *Utopia* to a so called college or university *educated* person, most of them either smile or chuckle as though you've made a funny joke.

Which reminds me of an interesting observation which I stumbled across.

It began when I went a few years without watching mainstream television.

Meanwhile it was just after 9/11 and I was educating myself through reading non-fiction and watching documentaries, etc.

So after mainlining reality for a couple years, I moved to a new residence where I was once again exposed to mainstream programming such as prime time sitcoms.

Holy crap!

What I recognized instantly was that there was a direct connection between what was made to be the subject of their jokes and what we now see, over a decade later, as being things which certain organizations would prefer to belittle and suppress.

For me it was literally like okay here's another joke, so let's think about why they're making the effort to discredit this topic.

Like I said before, you can learn a lot about someone by what they choose to lie about.

Anyway back to my previous topic, Utopia.

My first question is simply to ask what we really have to lose by trying to get organized (for lack of a better term) with others around the block and the world?

I remember writing something years ago which seems fitting today, "Expecting it to be hard has prepared for it to now seem normal."

One thing to be clear about is that there will be things which we can instantly do without.

Propaganda, intrusive surveillance, unnecessary medications, etc.

Of course many of the usual tactics will be used by those unwilling to relinquish the control over others which they now have (and enjoy).

Once again I point out that slavery was never really eradicated.

There are actually still huge amounts of people enduring slavery to this day.

Not to mention all the other imposed controls which are becoming more apparent everyday for those willing to look past their self-centred apathy.

Obviously a better world is a long-term goal and getting the baby boomers to change at this point is rather unrealistic.

So one thing which would help ensure some major improvements is a complete overhaul of the *education* system.

Most parents would agree and most are now only dissuaded by how much they are told it would cost them.

Which is another reason why this whole idea needs to be global.

Because a lot of these subcategories have been tried in the past.

And what happened was that they were perceived as a threat to some global corporation etc, which in turn went to war with the idea and used whatever means were at its disposal.

So for example when we are told that something such as an improved education system would cost too much...

Well then with the global financial reach of some of these corps, it isn't hard to find a way to put financial pressure on the area that dared to give a shit about its kids.

A bit like the hammer finding the nail which stood out.

Which in turn reinforces the position of the apathetic masses who respond with terms like, "See, I told you nothing would change."

However with a large sustained, global, multilevel, peaceful, progressive, unwavering, inclusive...

Well then, I'm game.

Do you want to play?

We Are Told

We are told that life isn't fair.
We are told to keep our heads down.
We are told not to stick our necks out.
Did you ever stop listening to them?
Did you ever challenge the party line?
Then what happened?
Were you ignored, ridiculed, or even heard?
How far down the rabbit hole did you get?
How many tangents delayed your efforts?
Were you strong, steadfast, and did you have the pure intention to help
navigate you through the tests of integrity?
Ya, sweet.
Did you ever wonder how many of us survived?
I wonder about that a lot lately.
I mean really, one against those who use their power without challenge...
Shit, another lamb for the slaughter, right?!
But with numbers, well that's another story.
History is on our side and those numbers show an inevitable positive
outcome.
Never give up but recognize that we aren't perfect or 100% true in our
understanding.
One of my favourite philosophies is to err on the side of love.
No bullshit, let's strive for sustainable truth!

Wouldn't It Be Nice

"All of these skills... I will put in my back pocket... which I can make money off of...", she said.

Wouldn't it be nice to overhear a conversation involving a selfless act of kindness or a discussion about ways to make things better for everyone?

But alas, most of what I hear these days is bitching and plotting in this selfish clique reality.

We could spend time reminiscing about how we got into this mess.

And eventually someone would rewrite a history book or produce a sanitized film in which the characters with the most cash in real life come out as the heroes.

Blah, blah, blah, have another drink, smoke another joint, tune out, and try to forget that you made that conscious choice.

No worries, you've been taught to only care about you and yours.

Don't think about the innocent people killed today with your tax dollars.

Don't think about the poison you've been feeding yourself and your children.

Don't think *too much* or you might not pay your bills and then things can't stay the same.

For goodness sake don't change anything.

You might risk losing your significant other, your status at work, your this, your that, your selfish mother fucking life!

Come on, is it really that great?

The thrill of living in fear should have worn off by now.

Or maybe your role is to be beholden to a master.

You don't believe that you are deserving of this or that.

Well my friend, you are probably as deserving as most of the rest of us.

As a society we have supposedly agreed upon a number of laws.

So if you haven't broken the big ones recently, then learn from your mistakes and get back in the game.

When our delusions of reality become diluted and we are able to peer briefly out of this murky cesspool, "Well shit son!" it's not a matter of what you want.

It's a matter of a new kind of matter that you haven't even dreamt of yet.

Are you ready for something more and to make the transition from 2d to 3D with atmosphere.

They say there's no time like the present and sure there are a multitude of distractions to put off doing something new, until tomorrow.

"...creeping in this petty pace from day to day..."

Pop quiz, why are you here?

I'm really asking, what is the purpose of your life?

Did you ever have one or more than one?

If you are doing it now, great.

If not, what's stopping you?

In that case the odds are that your life has become self-defeating, you are your own worst enemy, etc.

Now usually come the excuses:

"But I must provide for my children (wife, husband, mother, father)."

"I just need to get my bills caught up before I can..."

"My meds are expensive."

"My life is a compromise and my job pays for my hobbies."

Doesn't anyone feel a duty to society or humanity for that matter?

The answer to that question is in general quite disturbing.

How did we get this way?

Well damn that's a big one, put the coffee on...

Maybe not today then, we'll get back to that at another time.

Let's just agree for now that the Machiavelli playbook is working overtime. The basic idea (for those who don't know) is to keep the *peasants* busy fighting each other so that they don't get organized and overthrow the crown (or the modern equivalent).

It really doesn't matter for the moment why we are being manipulated.

Just grab hold of your sanity and "sanitize that shit".

Purge your unwanted programming and run a virus scan.

Retrain yourself, freeing yourself from the electronic (subliminal) propagandas.

Reclaim your life, knowing that only a solid you can create something true.

Really question in the extreme where you are getting your info to make your daily decisions.

Honestly critically think about *little* things like what really were the agendas of the textbooks you were made to learn in school.

Or who really benefits from nothing ever changing politically, no matter who we vote for and elect.

Yes those are deeply complicated topics and on your own it would take quite some time for each nugget of info.

But there are more of us out there than is immediately apparent.

The real trick to master here is to find ways of networking without being intercepted, monitored, or overheard.

It will become increasingly obvious that the real reason for the *War on Terror* is to maintain the stranglehold that the invisible elite has on us peasants.

By labelling every gathering of two or more citizens who have the gall to question the authority of their masters, a possible terrorist threat.

What if most millionaires weren't isolated success stories, or if most militant racists weren't *lone nuts*, or if most disorganized criminals weren't *quite* so disorganized?

Yup a pretty bold (if not suicidal) statement would be to suggest in most of the above cases that those players are playing for the same team.

And they're definitely not The Avengers.

Okay consider that for a bit seriously, and let it sink in...

Running The Show

So let's discuss a point of view which I don't hear expressed very often.
We as a society seem to have this collective belief that those *running the show* are in control so completely that they can push through programs of mass surveillance, mass drugging of populations with food additives and anti-depressants, the suppression of technology and energy alternatives, etc. I hear you, I really do.

But the more that I dug into those and other activities of the *global evil empire*, the more I began to realize that those are actually the desperate calculated acts of an empire in decline.

You see, many of the ideas which *The Hippies, New Agers, and Seekers in the Now* have put forward in hopes of saving us from ourselves are in fact very powerful raw ideas.

But it is a bit like an average citizen attempting to sue a big corporation.
In that case, the citizen is usually bankrupted as the many corporate lawyers drag out the proceedings for years using every trick in the book.

Whereas in this case we are dealing with a war of propaganda, counter-intelligence, intimidation, ridicule, etc.

Once again I point out a situation which I call the dormant love potential in each of us.

You see the tricks and lies used by the adversary are quite cleaver like the Wolf dressed up as Granny.

And even more clever are the *true believers* who are sent out to con other defenceless consumers.

How many of you are aware of the psychological experiments conducted by the Nazis and other immoral historical organizations?

If you (that is they) can control the environment in which a society of humans lives, then you can condition them to accept and even participate in previously unimaginable horrors.

And we're not talking about a horror movie where everything is resolved in two hours and then you go back to bitching about that person who you are really jealous of but feel better *cuz u dissed them* to others laughter.

No, here we are talking about a long-term sustained effort.

Consider for a moment that we aren't living up to our potential as a species. I know not much of a stretch there.

But what if those yearned for abilities were more than just comic book daydreams?

Someone once mentioned to me that anything we can think of either existed once, exists now, or will exist.

The idea being that people aren't really that original and our thoughts are more like recollections.

So I think we have experienced or imagined enough of a humanity enslaved.

And the reason why it takes a sustained external negative effort to prevent us from fashioning the positive raw ideas into lasting peace, truth, and life...

Why it is love of course, our default position.

Most babies aren't born angry, fearful, and war-like.

It takes a lot of time and energy to keep humanity in a state of constant desperate struggle.

If you take the time to really understand the origins and motives of groups of people and why they fight and struggle with other groups, you will find in most cases that the persons involved were manipulated into no-win scenarios in which one person or group is forced to make a choice which either negatively affects them or the person or group that they are at odds with.

Ultimately this causes resentment and *bad blood* between the two groups which will continue to fester like an infection unless the truth is revealed and aired out.

So in this way we can see humanity metaphorically as a body on life support with never-ending multiple infections in which the body heat is used as a source of power for our isolated elite overlords.

Well today I am personally giving them notice.

Humanity's love will always find a way to triumph and the truth will always win.

Fish Out Of Water

So like George Michael said, "...I guess we should be praying for time..."

It's always a bad sign when you see the warlords laughing in public.

And when America's presidential election is so ridiculously pointless, well what are we to take from that?

As a Canadian, I am currently encouraged by the polling numbers indicating that a *change* is coming for us.

But of course, there are at least two major points to keep in mind.

The first one being that in comparison to our southern neighbours we are rather small in so many ways that one wonders if changing the *ruling* party and Prime Minister will have much of a positive effect at all.

And second does the government actually do any real governing, or is it more of a case of front line damage control for the corporatocracy?

Will any of the leaders seeking my vote actually pledge to be held accountable for their campaign promises and their actions if elected to office?

And if they actually did make that pledge, could we actually take them seriously?

But that in itself is small in comparison to the massive job of reversing the long-term effects which corporate politics has had on my country.

Then again how can a party get elected, or even more, get a majority government running on a platform of transparency and accountability when it costs so much money to plan and execute an effective campaign.

That money has to come from somewhere and it certainly isn't coming without strings attached.

And is it possible for the official opposition to take office (should they be elected) without being overwhelmed by the influences of the power brokers who seem to have their lackeys (oops, I mean associates) in all the key places?

It reminds me of an elite equestrian jumping course, with a pressing time limit and consistently harder jumps to complete just to keep from being disqualified.

Okay let's set aside the extremely low odds of success and instead turn our attention towards the goals and objectives of this *fantasy* scenario.

We'll start with some realistic short-term initial goals and expand the scope to include more difficult long-term objectives.

How about the gradual elimination of useless time consuming chores like driving and maintaining your vehicle, washing your dishes and household chores, yard maintenance and household garbage collecting/sorting?

When I was a teenager reading science fiction, those bright minds were showing us a future where technology would make our lives easier and a world that would come to realize the futility of wars.

Well as a species, we have proven time and again that we can achieve anything we put our minds to.

Unless of course some of *us* are actually impeding, suppressing, or disappearing some of the crucial efforts needed to get from here to there.

Yes I know, I'm being *paranoid* or I "just don't understand the reality of the situation", right?

Well I'm past the point where ridicule has much of an impact.

Truly through the many years in which I have been concerned with humanity's plight, there have been numerous times where I have attempted to settle for and even accept the simpler and more sane solutions.

But alas they never really stuck.

You see, when a person turns off the TV and reduces their exposure to the multitude of subliminal propaganda from other areas.

And instead tries to live their life in a state of healthy (for lack of a better term) awareness of our past, present, and future.

Well, it is a bit like a fish out of water.

Once you learn to breathe on dry land, sure you go back into the water to visit, but land becomes a whole new adventure which also teases access to the air and outer space.

But that isn't something we are supposed to spend much time considering.

It really is staggering how little progress *we* have made since the moon landing.

We have been conditioned to believe that space is mostly unattainable and fraught with danger, not to mention those evil aliens waiting to gobble us up.

I would start by saying that, at the very least, space has been privatized.

Or I could say poetically that, "Heaven has been sold and we're not invited."

But don't take my word for it, do your own investigations or go back to sleep...

Joffrey's Fall

Okay, so it turns out that politics sucks ass.

You see, the month or so run up to the election gives the corporate spin doctors plenty of time to raise enough divisive issues to sway the final outcome in the desired direction.

There are so many polls going on constantly that it really is a *no-brainer*. And since *obviously* the desired group is already in power and has been for quite some time now, the only real opportunity for a change of leadership would be if those in power were to mess up so bad that their public opinion plummets below 20% and no amount of spin could pull them out of their free-fall.

Contributing to this dilemma is the three party system which we Canadians currently *enjoy*.

One point which I made on Facebook is that the reason why the current *ruling* party had enough votes to get elected initially and continues to get re-elected is that they are in fact the result of combining two previously competing parties.

So how do we get the two competing second and third place parties to find enough common ground to work together over the remaining days and find a way to take the throne from *Joffrey?*

One possible solution could be to get them to agree to share power for the next five year term with the understanding that they will return to being competing parties at term's end.

Of course I personally have a preference as to which of those two I am voting for but I also believe that either one is better than the party currently in power.

There is a saying that a long journey begins with a single step and I believe that we have a good general idea of the direction to face.

Now it is up to us to take that first step.

I'm not really sure that it matters all that much which of those two leaders takes that first step so long as they are supported, encouraged, and advised on the following journey.

The major dilemma as I see it, is that both leaders are very strong personalities and getting them to become subordinate to the other would be a tough sell.

So what if we get them to agree to a neutral figure head which would allow them both to *keep face* and thereby maintain their equality in this temporary union?

Must the opposition parties remain fragmented into inconsequential pieces? Furthermore, a makeshift alliance would prepare those leaders and their parties for a leadership role in global organizations such as the UN.

Let's return our country to a situation where we are often times setting positive presidents for others to follow.

And let us not delude ourselves into believing that we are unique in our ingenuity.

Don't get me wrong, I'm a proud Canuck.

But the more I see of other cultures, the more I believe we have to learn from each other.

And it is more important now than ever before to find common ground globally and work together.

"Surely you must be joking!", you say.

Not at all, I am simply reiterating a statement which has been used numerous times by a wide variety of political animals.

The difference being the reason why I am saying it.

As always, intention is key to getting positive results.

In my case, I am not asking for you to give me your power and make you promises that I will never keep.

But rather my objective is as it has always been, to empower you and everyone equally.

Some of the people who hear me, say that they don't think we should empower the *bad folks*.

Once again, what we are dealing with is a misunderstanding of *empowerment*.

You see the empowerment that I am talking about is to be so full of love that you have enough for yourself and those around you.

"But what is love anyway?", you ask.

Finally a good topic for in depth discussion...

The Good Fight

Money.

Need I say more?

That's ultimately what it came down to once again.

Yes, I'm still talking politics.

It has been a final blitz of exaggerated claims.

Pandering to separate demographics, each party attempts to scare the voters into believing that there is only one choice for that individual's financial well being.

And since we've all given up on political long-term promises, we take the money and run.

Collectively believing those *little white lies* and keeping our fingers crossed that things will be better tomorrow.

With our short attention spans not many of us have really acknowledged that the proverbial frog has been boiling in that pot for quite a while now.

When I point out that people appear to be ailing more and more these days, the deniers talk about life spans getting longer.

So to that I reply that what I'm talking about is quality of life and being doped up, biopsied, and radiated for the final decade isn't much of a trade-off.

Not to mention all those medical bills which financially rape the victims and their families.

But as a Commonwealth country we are supposed to keep a stiff upper lip, right?

And the actual numbers of people suffering verses those apparent on the surface is a rather large margin.

See the whole board people!

I remember an old black and white Outer Limits or Twilight Zone episode where the protagonist gets trapped in a small town while the inhabitants are driven crazy one-by-one as the meaning of life is passed around in a whisper.

Ignorance is bliss, so fucking true.

But am I seeing our future or is it just wishful thinking on my part?

Patience is a virtue.

So should I put down the pen and picket sign and try to find some harmless distractions while the hoped for pieces fall into place?

I gotta say that the odds of that happening on my part are pretty slim.

Sitting on the sidelines for so long waiting for the coach to put me in.

Fuck that!

No more waiting, like Melissa Etheridge wrote, "We are the ones we've been waiting for."

So the time for keeping quiet and trying not to be noticed is over.

But that does not mean that raging around like a child throwing a temper tantrum is a good option.

It is so easy to distort the truth in the court of public opinion that it is vitally important to exemplify the virtues that we are extolling.

Practice what you preach!

I have used myself as a test balloon recently, being open about how I feel and wearing Wikileaks supportive clothing.

Still walkin' and talkin' brothers and sisters.

Sure there are fringe beliefs that each of us has but the things that we need to fight for collectively are the big ideas which we all share.

As I have spoken about previously, at length, first we need to agree on the necessary changes to the system.

Then come the implementations and once some stability is achieved again, proceed to do more of the big changes systematically.

So obviously patience is key while maintaining focus on the big picture.

It's probably a good time to get out the old pad and paper.

Make a list of what is most important to you and then try to rank the list in order from most important to least.

Of course this is only a preliminary draft which can be added to or subtracted from.

The main point is to have something which you can go back to as a reminder and also to expand upon.

These ideas are emotional and it is easy to get lost in other people's persuasions.

So think about this like volunteering with the option to turn it into a career. Or look at it like a rental which you have the option to buy.

Now comes a personal warning from my own experience.

There are plenty of reasons why there aren't any reliable handbooks for what we are trying to do.

Off the top of my head, I'll throw a few out there.

Maybe there will be one or two that you forgot about or hadn't connected the dots to.

Hell if you've read the rest of my writing, you probably are aware of many that I don't.

Nazi International, Catholic Church, Big Oil, Big Pharma, International Banking Cartels, and corporations too numerous to name individually.

Okay that's enough.

Now I'm not saying that any of these are consciously connected, although I wouldn't be the least bit surprised.

But they all stand to benefit in various ways by keeping the 99% poor and isolated.

If you really look at it with an open mind, you would see that it really isn't that hard for them to, "pin-point potential trouble-makers and neutralize them."

What with those mandatory twelve years of *schooling* and all the tests and assessments.

If you thought the politicians had an unfair advantage with the numerous custom-tailored polls and virtually unlimited funds from their corporate backers.

Consider what our *permanent records* tell our overlords about our *potential*. And there is the old saying about keeping your friends close and your enemies closer.

I will leave the tools and manipulations to your imagination but at the end of the day the percentages of us *trouble-makers* are really quite low and easily marginalized.

Remember the good fight is a long one.

Plot Twist

Okay, so we kicked Joffrey off the throne.

So now what?

Time for a new poll.

How many people who voted Liberal really expect PM Justin to fulfill the majority of his campaign promises?

And while he attempts to mobilize the people for change, we still need to reverse the negative effects that the last decade of Conservative rule has had on the country.

Don't get me wrong, overall I am optimistic for our little country.

But one huge potential issue could be if we are drawn into another 9/11 type situation where the USA is once again attacked or perceived to have been attacked.

We need to make it crystal clear that our support for their imperial conquest is not automatic.

Also, another major issue towards independence is that we are a resource rich country with a huge chunk of land and vast coastal waters.

We need to stand up for the real value of Canada on the world market.

"Expecting it to be hard, has prepared for it to now seem normal."

And we will embrace the inclusiveness that is our country at its best.

Imagine the potential of a new batch of students with cultural influences from every part of the world.

No more disregarding potential energy alternatives to protect Big Oil.

Sure the empire to the south will initially frown on our newly claimed independence.

But when you look around the world, you will eventually notice that many other countries have been pioneering many of these ideas for years.

If the USA slowly sheds its multitude of well cultivated fears and slowly begins the journey out of its isolationist need to control every other country on the planet...

Well then, eventually even the bully falls in love.

And I'm not talking about a short-term infatuation or an intoxicating addiction.

What if in spite of the monstrous imperial power grab that is the recent USA, the rest of the planet found peace, serenity, and financial security.

Damn, now wouldn't that be attractive?

Down right sexy.

That certainly would be an interesting plot twist.

Like a biker with an abusive childhood, eventually he has to burn the leather and rejoin humanity.

No it won't be easy but totally doable.

Remember ultimately we are all one family and a good talk, a few tears, and a hug can work wonders.

Time for a new chapter...

Change Of Management

As the victory celebrations wind down, reality sets in and we start to recognize that there is no quick fix for our economic short-comings, racial divides, or our follower status on the world stage.

Sure it is fun to believe that a change of leadership one day will instantly transform our fortunes.

But alas the legacy of our enslaving economic, toothless political, and decapitated religious systems quickly dispel such fantasies.

And all of these are enforced by the hired gun gangsters who live for the moment and have no allegiance to anything but their next paycheck.

This road has been a long one and, briefly stated, what has been happening is that power has been seized by multiple groups on multiple fronts.

Meanwhile many hard-working well-intentioned individuals do what they can to make the most of a deteriorating situation.

They are truly heroes to whom we owe a great deal.

I don't want to think about where we would be without them.

And occasionally someone like John Lennon, Martin Luther King, or JFK comes along in the right position at the right time.

We all know what happened to them.

There were also thousands more people with similar intentions and talents but for various reasons they weren't able to realize their life's goals.

From my perspective I can see a variety of weapons that were not only possibly used against these potential pioneers but many that have been acknowledged as being used successfully in the past.

Which brings up another problem that we face when attempting to combat this empire of chaos.

Because our society and environment are constantly changing, so the weapons used against us are constantly adapting in their stealth capabilities.

Shit, I just realized that this must seem either utterly overwhelming or completely insane.

Which is probably why I feel compelled to share it.

The two most common responses that I get from those who take the time to voice a response are either rather simplistic sound bytes which they have heard somewhere else or various brief attempts at persuading me of the futility of my pursuits.

But lately no one has really taken the time to have a constructive dialogue.

I am now past the point of trying to guilt people into action.

The ones I am speaking to now are those who feel that the cause which they are a part of now isn't effecting the change that they had hoped for.

Instead of joining a group which was started by someone with too much time and money on their hands, why not try to build something from the ground up with like-minded others?

From what I can see, at this point our best tactic is that of transparency and exposure, at least for those of us living in Canada and the USA.

Maybe elsewhere as well but as I am located in Canada, that is the environment which I am most acquainted with.

At this point with organizations like Wikileaks exposing more and more leaked documents pertaining to abuses of power by governments, corporations, and intelligence agencies, there are a large number of people who are angry and looking for legitimate ways to affect a positive change.

So it is imperative to not give the spin doctors ammunition to discredit a valid cause.

Therefore angry violent rhetoric has no place in a positive movement.

Remember what happened at the WTO protests of the past, where a few agent provocateurs turned a good demonstration into a joke with one violent outburst.

Of course there are numerous stumbling blocks on the road from chaos to serenity and one of the largest preventing others from joining in is simply proving to them that our vision of the future is in fact possible.

Another easily manipulated issue is the whole debate surrounding the legalization of drugs.

There are so many opinions on this one topic that it has become the ultimate divisive issue.

Similar to the gay marriage debate, this one issue becomes a never-ending Jerry Springer show.

Personally I have experienced many of the points of view at different times in my life.

At this point my view is that more harm is done by banning the substances themselves.

I am not saying that getting high is a positive recreational activity but by criminalizing it we push the whole culture underground and that has far worse consequences than the alternatives.

But really what people choose to do to their bodies is their business.

I am more concerned with what some people feel that they have the right to do to others.

That is where the laws are supposed to step in and protect those who can't defend themselves.

Instead the current system spends a lot of time dictating and monitoring what the average peasant is allowed to do to themselves in the (supposed) privacy of their own home.

Don't get me wrong, as defensive corporate strategies go it is quite brilliant.

But now that we have a change of management in the PM's office, maybe we could do some real governing again.

Anyway, just a thought...

Top Three

All quiet on the western front.
Or should I say all is pacified, medicated, and deceived?
On the surface our western *Christian* dominated society seems to have adopted the same painted face facade as the celebrities we worship.
A simplistic sound byte from my perspective is that we follow our various rule books which all have similar basic frameworks.
"Be good, respect authority, and you will be rewarded in the afterlife."
The perfect doctrine of control instilling guilt and fear based on misguided faith.
The beautiful thing about this system is that there is no way to disprove the foundation that holds up its menagerie.
And so long as the true reality of the zoo which we inhabit is kept from the majority, we will continue to elect different flavoured puppets and then bitch and moan when things not only do not get better but the problems actually begin to expand exponentially.
Yup I know, certainly not an inspiring happy fuzzy get well card.
This isn't a situation where getting a good night's sleep, taking your vitamins and drinking lots of fluids is going to do much except allow us to tread water in reality's river as humanity rushes steadily towards another waterfall.
I sometimes get discouraged by the new crop of twenty-somethings I see poised to take the reins.
It seems like the only thing that they learned in school was how to not get caught by the teacher.
Oh sure occasionally there is an online *cause of the day*.
But I rarely see well informed movements with positive long-term planning.
Their generally short attention spans and lack of critical thinking have presented a long string of emotionally reactionary quick-fix short-term proposals.

These actions can't even be called solutions because if one pays attention to these issues following the brief flourishes of resolve, more often than not the results aren't much more than watered down compromises.

Even if the situations end well, more nightmares inevitably ensue when it comes to trying to enforce the newly proposed changes.

Once again, I am not trying to discourage people from making the effort.

Just hoping that I can encourage them to aim higher.

Consider that a city can't effectively go to war against a country.

That city is easily encircled and overwhelmed.

So it is that we have to be not only prepared to fight for our impending freedom on multiple fronts but we have to actively search out each struggle.

And a reactionary struggle will always be one step behind.

We need to be self-determining.

Once again a disclaimer for the haters, when I say *fight* I am not encouraging violence.

Quite the opposite, for the battles that we fight are humanitarian and idealistic, aimed at making violence an unthinkable memory of the past.

We should not sway from our commitment and resolve.

Not let emotion cloud our common sense.

And while events like the Paris attacks are aimed at producing desired reactions in various people, certainly we should be the best of neighbours and friends.

But in these situations it is important to not fall into the traps laid by the same barbarians who orchestrated the horrors.

Obviously we need to take time to mourn, but follow that by strengthening our resolve to continue on our path.

If we simply perpetually retaliate like Israel and Palestine, all that happens is that we make the holes we are both in deeper.

In any situation which requires a solution I attempt to search out the root causes.

Many people aren't going to want to hear my next comparison but the conflict with ISIS in a lot of ways resembles the IRA conflict with England.

The NATO countries claim to be the defenders of righteousness and we claim that we are standing up against aggression.

But the ISIS situation is the product of our own aggression coming back to haunt us.

Yes I know, the whole situation is remarkably complex.

Ultimately it doesn't much matter any more who started what or whether we've killed more than them.

Women, children, genocide, war crimes, political bullshit, religious extremists...

Hell, we could put all those who are guilty on the Jerry Springer show and that Special Presentation would run for centuries.

But no amount of justice and accountability can bring the victims back from their graves.

Like the scourge of Nazism we should be aware of and remember our mistakes and those of others.

But when you weigh the pros and cons one way or the other, it will be far more beneficial to simply move on and let bygones be bygones.

Realistically nothing is holding us back more than the fear of prosecution by the so-called leaders of many of the factions at play.

Kind of like the old IRA saying, "We can defeat the English authority by simply ignoring it."

All these petty wars are like attempts at distracting us from the fact that peace is just up ahead so long as we get there before we blow ourselves up.

If you can look past the *riddles and confusion*, you can unravel the *truth delusion*.

Like John Lennon said, let us imagine.

What if we got everyone to pause at the same time and really search themselves.

Then write down their top three needs for this life!

And cross reference those results in one of those NSA supercomputers.

Seven billion people surveyed and the top three answers on the board...

Doomsday

Okay, so it's all fucked up.

But you don't want to hear it.

Hell, it's only a month till Christmas.

So let's all be neighbourly, drink, and be merry.

I remember all those strange questions we used to ask when we were drinking, getting high, or just having a coffee and a smoke.

You know the ones that get dismissed by someone saying, "Who knows?!"

Well what if you started getting the answers to those questions?

And what if you didn't have anything holding you back from putting the pieces together?

How many people would be crazy or stupid enough to follow through?

I'll wager not many.

And what would really be the point?

Is it possible that having the whole picture would present as being believable?

Would you just end up being that person sitting alone on the park bench laughing sporadically for no apparent reason?

Or maybe it would be so overwhelming that you would slip into a depression so deep that self medication would be your final solution.

Either way leading a productive life would become less of an option.

So how to muddle through?

There's strength in numbers, but there's the rub!

Since any meeting of people with those beliefs would definitely be flagged as a threat by Homeland Security.

So personally I have chosen to be open about how I feel while at the same time making it clear that my views are in no way supportive of violence in any form.

And while the mass public are spoon fed bits and pieces, like the fact that Hitler probably survived the war.

Most of the critical info surrounding the hows and whys are either glossed over or outright omitted.

This is for various reasons.

For example, how long would the History Channel stay on the air if they got too close to uncovering the real power structures governing our present reality?

It's fine to speculate on events from 70 years ago, but not to suggest that the main Fascist players from the war weren't defeated so much as they disappeared into the scenery in a pre-planned effort.

World domination was actually never the goal of WW2 for the Nazis.

It was more like a power grab and the greatest heist in recorded history.

And they sold their propaganda so well that many of those who were victimized fought to the end in defence of a Fuhrer who had already flown the coop.

In the end it was like a global doomsday cult with a twist, the top inner circle escaped with the loot.

But of course the Nazis weren't the last to strip mine a society of its wealth.

Methods vary but the Fascist Hall of Infame continues to grow.

And more regular folk would recognize the extent of the deception if the banks and corporations which control the research and production of the *latest and greatest* technology weren't owned by these same Fascist banksters.

It is sad to think that most people really believe that public figures like Bill Gates, Steve Jobs, and Mark Zuckerberg are the pioneers guiding us into a new frontier.

Believe this my friends.

We are being spoon fed the technologies which are enslaving and brainwashing us.

In much the same way that we are being manipulated into accepting more Fascist laws every day.

Put it this way, if it is a plot for a Hollywood film, it probably has plenty of truth to it.

So as always the point of this particular public service announcement is to help inform more people of the reality of the situation so that they can then make better decisions as to our collective future.

We all as one are an amazing mosaic.

With our collective input we can ultimately decide how to wrest power from the machines, be they physical or bureaucratic.

And when the common citizen is treated as a family member instead of a farm animal, slave, or indentured servant.

And when we can return to a time when things can be passed down from one generation to another, instead of having to sell the whole estate to get grandma into a *nice* nursing home.

It is said that it takes a village to raise a child.

Well I would say that it takes a majority of the planet's population being educated in a truthful and nurturing environment over a sustained period to begin to repair the gaping wounds inflicted upon countless victims.

I am counting on you all...

That's The Shit

So you believe that you've outsmarted the bastards, hey?

Not even close to being true.

Think of it this way.

In a world of focus groups, online surveys, and NSA sponsored meta-data collection...

If there is a large sum of money involved then there is an even larger idea involved, guaranteed.

And just because an idea is big doesn't mean that it is good.

These days the real wars aren't reported on the nightly news broadcasts.

And while television police dramas and *common* sense have trained us to follow the money in order to discover who benefits from a crime, there are deeper levels of finance than the ones which even most cops have access to.

And with revelations about the PROMIS software (Prosecutor's Management Information System) which was distributed and installed worldwide on countless financial systems, it is apparent that the built-in back doors would allow not only the monitoring of financial transactions but also the manipulation of the actual numbers themselves.

So to understand the truly clandestine exchanges we need to go back to the old school of cloak and dagger meetings in person for the real deals.

Of course there may be more advanced untraceable tech involved but not likely.

So the next time a major crime is committed and the trail seems a little too easy to follow, think about it.

Which brings us back to the non-stop news coverage of individuals killing individuals and groups killing groups.

Obviously (to me anyway), the purpose behind the group efforts (whether government or terrorist) is to affect changes.

Now whether those changes are ones of public opinion or simply to do away with their perceived enemies is of course different for each instance.

And when we really critically examine the motives behind the apparently isolated attacks by one or two people we will begin to see patterns.

But like observing the behaviours of subatomic particles, certain tools need to be either created or made available.

Not only do we need to be able to change our perception from the macro to the micro but also from the visible spectrum to the otherwise unseen frequencies.

I would suggest that, at the moment, most people are making judgments and assumptions based on dangerously insufficient data.

Which is of course why so many people simply give up and focus on their own families and other things which they have some measure of control over.

I definitely understand that it can be overwhelming to peer behind the curtain for the first time.

I have been pulling back the curtain periodically for years now and some days are sure challenging.

But what it comes down to, like so many challenges in life, is love.

I know it sounds silly but persistence, understanding, stubbornness, dedication, etc are all well and good however fleeting states of mind.

But real love is eternal and unwavering.

And when the ramifications of not doing anything to curtail our further enslavement are made clear...

Well then you will discover that to protect your family and whatever else you hold dear...

"Truth shall not be sold in flavours."

For example *terrorism* has been used for the last 15 years (post 9/11) as an excuse to mass surveil the entire population of the planet.

But if the above stated organized effort by those in the shadows is even moderately true, how can we possibly fight back?

Think about it, mass movements require money and organization.

Which are the very things which the *intelligence* communities are heavily monitoring.

The only other organizations which are successfully staying off the radar are the drug cartels but they are actually a separate department of the elite control system.

Once again, consider this...

When was the last time you or anyone you know has had an hour or more of really free time?

And when you are *free* are you also free from intoxicants (drugs, alcohol, tobacco, caffeine)?

I didn't think so.

We are sold the idea that we occasionally deserve a break.

But we aren't expected to actually have a prolonged period of deep thought.

No, the idea of a break in pop culture is to have a _____ (fill in the blank with some product, glass of wine, coffee, smoke, etc).

The only sustained periods of deep thought which are acceptable are when we contemplate a politically correct method of making our day to day enslavement more tolerable.

But heaven forbid that we question the underlying paradise which was sold to us as our desire.

So turn off your phone more often and detox from those *mood altering* substances.

Give that a month or so and begin to contemplate what your life could and should be like and about.

It is really about being able to see the forest from the trees and recognizing that you are that frog in the pot of boiling water.

Understanding how you got there isn't as immediately important as removing yourself from that situation sooner rather than later.

Like an abuse victim, you won't immediately recognize your true value until you start to live without fear.

No fear, that's the shit!

Enterprise

So apparently the bastards did it again.

Another mass shooting.

I know what else is new, right?

The San Bernardino shooting is being sold to us as a couple of radicalized Muslims in the good old USA.

But once again if we are patient and dig a little deeper, the truth really is far different.

Instead of two brown skin Muslims, we should apparently be looking for three Caucasian mercenaries.

They were described by eyewitnesses as fleeing the crime scene in a black SUV.

Meanwhile the mainstream press tell us that the perpetrators were in fact a husband and wife team who were found handcuffed to the inside of their vehicle, *already dead*.

Some astute people who were paying attention have pointed out that earlier in the day Russia had presented strong evidence about the USA and its allies involved in the ISIS oil situation.

But don't worry about that, here's another mass shooting to distract us.

Don't you ever wonder why there isn't serious major investigations into why there are so many discrepancies in these so-called terrorist acts?

Yeah *who knows*, right?

Well someone certainly knows or else why would there not be more official investigations?

Some of us who have been attempting to get answers, have gotten a few but nowhere near a presentable picture.

Would it shock you to learn that the USA wasn't *The Ultimate Power In The Universe*?

What if there weren't categories like countries or job titles like president or CEO for those who are really running the show?

What if there were reasons other than national security for why we don't have flying cars, etc?

Are you comfortable perpetually living in the *Brave New World* of *1984*?

Have you even read *1984* the book, it is a must read?

Are you proud that you are raising your kids to be brainwashed ignorant slaves?

I am really not trying to guilt you into action, just reminding you of this reality.

Why not let the new Star Wars film inspire us to rebel against the real evil empire.

But wait, I forgot that this isn't a video game.

So there aren't any cheat codes to advance you to level 99 or make you indestructible.

I guess that means you are out then, hey?

Well don't say you weren't invited to the party.

So briefly what we are looking at is a multilevel criminal *Enterprise* the likes of which hasn't been seen before.

Their power can be seen on all levels from the street, to the underworld, to the highest echelons of the military industrial complex and of course the leaders of any country which they have interests in.

Yup, sounds insane and paranoid alright.

Once again I point out that I have been discussing these topics for years and the only other really plausible answer that I hear from people as to what's going on is...

Wait for it...

"People are inherently selfish, lazy, stupid, and violent."

Kind of sounds like the rhetoric used by the Nazis to dehumanize their enemies (Jews, Gays, Blacks, Communists, etc) in the eyes of their supporters.

Time for a group hug people, we need to work together or else.

What do you think the purpose of human life is?

Oops, I almost talked about religion there.

But we must not do that.

That is sacred ground after all.

Sometimes it is like we are living in the world of an Atari video game cartridge.

"Things are the way they are and that's that."

We are only allowed to play the game, not change the program.

Which of course makes sense since we are too *selfish, lazy, stupid, and violent* to create anything useful anyway.

So we must content ourselves with scraps from the master's table.

And enjoy the sense of usefulness we get from treating the victims of war and pollution.

What is it exactly that we are waiting for?

Do you think that things will get better all by themselves?

I understand that the propaganda is effectively confusing us to the point where even if someone was motivated enough to try earnestly to correct some problems they simply don't know where to start.

Like a leaky boat with multiple cracks in the hull, the first thing is to try to make it to shore so that it can be dry docked and repaired all at once.

But if we are all rowing in different directions, shore will have to wait.

And even if we make it to shore, the first thing that happens will be that a number of different people begin to fight over how to fix it and who should get paid to do the work.

Following this battle comes the battle for our sanity as the work gets indefinitely delayed and goes massively over budget.

When and if it ever gets completed, we end up with a pretty cool little ship that only the uber rich can afford tickets to ride.

I remember back in the day watching James Bond and WW2 films.

Good times, believing that the generals and intelligence agencies were fighting the good fight.

Sure is different from the corporate rat race we live in now, where the rats are looting the planetary sinking ship.

And all the while their propaganda tells the victimized mass populace that it's their own damn fault.

Yup it's our fault they hit us, we asked for it.

Bullshit!

The Thin Edge Of The Wedge

"So where's your proof?", said the closed-minded, Armageddon seeking, Nazi wannabe.

In my eyes the crazy world we live in is a pretty tangled web with trap doors, smoke, and mirrors.

To say the least.

But from the adversary's perspective it is a well-oiled machine with a web that is tightly strung and tuned to perfection.

I mean here's just one point that makes me want to smack some people across the face to wake them up.

The *Secret Space Program*.

People actually believe that trillions of dollars just disappear every year and NASA actually appears to get worse at its job.

Meanwhile we the public are expected to survive on 70 year old power plants, death-trap cars, poisonous food, etc.

Of course from my perspective this topic is entirely speculative, which is not to say that I am incorrect.

There is a scene in the film *Conspiracy Theory* where Mel Gibson's character is snatched up and held captive by the bad guys.

The one question that he keeps asking, because he raised so many issues involving conspiracies and the like, is "What did I get right?"

These days, back in the real world, the playbook for those who are involved in *black ops* is to simply deny everything.

You see, we have been conditioned to only believe information packaged and delivered in certain ways.

So while there are a number of good people out there trying to blow the whistle on various issues, unless it is presented in a big budget Hollywood film and spoon fed to us by an A-list celebrity then it simply isn't credible in the court of public opinion.

And even when the situation is laid out plain and simple, like the collapse of the housing market, the wagons circle around to protect the guilty parties.

This is ostensibly to prevent the thin edge of the wedge from penetrating the dam of power.

Oh sure there may occasionally be a sacrificial lamb tossed over the wall but it usually isn't anyone of any significance to the power structure.

Mainly because we the people doing all the real work are completely divorced from the employing and directing of our own armed forces in these times of actual immanent threat.

It sometimes seems like we are getting closer and closer to living in a global concentration camp.

The Nazis put the words "Work sets you free" at the entrances to many of their death camps.

Now we see those ideas used in countless advertising slogans.

Sure it isn't the same exact words and death doesn't come quite as quickly but they are getting more efficient every day.

I know, I know, this is the part where people get all upset about my comparison to our plight being similar to the victims of the Nazi's.

Pull your heads out of the sand and maybe you would begin to notice the similarities.

But that is ultimately your choice and you have all been subtly threatened in a multitude of ways about the penalties for questioning their *authority*.

Those threats are not only to you but also to your families.

Which brings me to an important issue and misconception in our time.

Back in the day there were local groups, gangs, and organizations which came into being to protect people in an area or neighbourhood from negative outside influences.

And while many of their activities were outside the law, for the most part there was a code of conduct.

No women, no kids.

Pretty simple really, keeping their *turf* safe like Al Pacino in The Godfather films.

But in the same way that big box stores put *mom and pop* stores out of business, these local gangsters have been replaced by *cartel franchises*.

The code has changed and the women and kids who aren't already on prescription pharmaceuticals are pressured into using gateway narcotics, as well as cigarettes and alcohol.

After all that's what all the cool people do in the movies and music videos. So after taking all that into consideration, why do I bother with talking about secret space programs, elite power hierarchies, and the general rotten-to-the-core corruption that wanders the streets in suits and drives Mercedes. Like I have said before, I do it because I can and because someone has to. You see there are so many examples both in the past and present of a downward slide in our general well being that it is getting to the point where my views are close to being outlawed.

Yup I know, there's that *unfounded* paranoia again.

So here's a thought exercise involving one potential future scenario.

Consider how advanced the real technologies are in those *black budget* research projects which have been going on since at least World War 2.

We in mainstream society keep plodding along with fossil fuel power sources to power our homes, cars, and planes.

Meanwhile our taxes, drug use, and arms sales are perpetually fuelling the underground research of continuously improving tech.

At some point we will become virtually incapable of defending ourselves from these new tech gods.

Like a religious person would say at that point we are then living *by the grace of god.*

Well I seem to remember that back in the Old Testament of the Christian Bible, occasionally god got mad at us.

And when you factor in that we have been conditioned for years to be fearful of an *alien invasion.*

What if it only seems like an attack from out of this world?

There would be no need for the Presidents and Prime Ministers to worry about getting permission for that war as they would have *plausible deniability.*

Not to mention all the pretty laboratory modified viruses and diseases which are getting stronger and more numerous every day.

Of course being a lowly slave myself, I can only speculate at their endgame. But things sure don't appear to be getting better anytime soon, unless...

The choice is as it always has been, ours together.

IV

The Truth Will Out

War in pieces.

Petrodollars have been ruling the global economy for decades.

But some countries with brave leaders have tried to take a stand.

Although none of them were angels by any means, I mourn their passing and thank them for helping to increase awareness of the struggle.

When I was a kid, I played a board game called Risk with my friends.

Of course there were other games like Monopoly and Chess but Risk was our favourite and for good reason.

You see the goal of the game was global domination and its rules and method of play were simple enough for kids to play.

"Everybody wants to rule the world."

But back to our present reality, we have psychotic movers and shakers with no checks and balances other than public awareness.

Once again, normal folks like you and me outnumber the assholes by at least 50 to 1.

And some of us tech-savoy kids tricked the powers-that-be into allowing us to build the internet.

What it boiled down to was that their greed got the better of them.

And they couldn't imagine a beast that they couldn't bring to heal.

You see this pattern repeated numerous times throughout history.

Simplified it is a pyramid structure with a megalomaniac at the top, starting the pattern.

They use all their tools of deception to build an ironclad inner circle who are then sent out to further the growth of the beast.

And this continues on and on and on...

But like the party game Telephone, the indoctrination gets more diluted as it gets further from the dictator.

So that in this case we have a technologically dominant society ruled by a group who really don't understand how the tech works.

And there are numerous examples through history but the one which springs to my mind is the prisoners of war in Nazi Germany who found ways of sabotaging the weapons and tech which they were forced to work on.
Nowadays, they are trying to find ways to get around the complete shutdown of the beast.
Redundancy is the name of this game.
With mass media propaganda unleashed to perfection, the modern slaves have been persuaded to build the tools of their own enslavement.
But once again the pesky problem of that global population is getting in the way of a nice quiet domination.
Which is the main reason we have seen a major shift towards drones and cybernetics.
Full definition of *cybernetics*: The science of communication and control theory that is concerned especially with the comparative study of automatic control systems (as the nervous system and brain and mechanical-electric communication systems).
All right then, that should be enough background for the moment.
So what can you and me do about this situation?
Well of course it is different for each of us.
But an important first step is to get the word out about the realities we are facing.
I cannot emphasize this enough.
No one will lift a finger to change anything unless they really believe that there is a problem.
And most people are happily floating down the river of high octane propaganda.
It tells them reassuring lies like the idea that those who challenge the reality sold to them by the corporations and religions are inferior, lazy, crazy, jealous, etc.

While at the same time convincing them that the reasons for their debts, cancers, ulcers, and autisms is due to their own sins in one form or another. Fear, the great equalizer.

And with the side effects of the various meds that most people are taking, the emotional roller coaster is a daily struggle.

No wonder most feel that their free moments need to be spent drinking, running, or some other *escape*.

Taking all this into account doesn't leave much time for civil resistance or to properly educate their children who are being indoctrinated into a wonderland the likes of which Alice would have had trouble with.

Waiting for someone else to save you or us?

Think about where that idea comes from.

Religion, politics, school, movies, etc.

And who were the money bags who had the final say as to what would be the final dogmas, film/TV scripts, and mottos?

Like I have said numerous times, corporations don't vote against their own interests.

And we are at the point now where if we are smart, determined, and in large numbers say that we have had enough...

We need to act sooner rather than later.

Do what you can but here is a huge point to remember.

Even if what you say is 95% true and only 5% is untrue, or worse absurd, then that is all anyone will remember.

So do your investigations and only speak up about what you know is 100% true.

The truth will out the bastards.

Everyday Paradox

The night always ends.
Every day is new.
I've learned to go with it.
Even when it's been a drag, love could be lurking around the corner.
Like a surprise party, sometimes it jumps out at you.
But don't jump back, lean forward and look it in the eyes.
Two fusion isotopes which are stable in isolation.
But get them together, wow!
I have become life the creator of worlds.
Suddenly life's deficits hold little power.
Universal DJ taking requests.
Or how about rock paper scissors for the next creation?
Just never let go, that's the promise.
Of course there is really no separation ever.
It's all just an illusion eliciting a response.
Enjoy the emotions but keep love on the throne.
I see infinity in her eyes.
And I will be her anything, everything, even nothing if needed.
Whatever it takes only limited by desire.
Struggling to be original but how to create a modern masterpiece about the most popular muse, love?
So let's go to warp speed through those heart shaped symbols...
Lay on your bed, put the posters on your walls, turn on the music and mood lighting.
Okay you feel me and now that feeling is my sanctuary.
I'm never really far from it, no matter what.
And my brain goes even deeper understanding that even if this particular relationship doesn't work out, it is the desire to share time with another that matters.
Whatever that looks like, let's be original and experience something new.
Okay suppose all good things come to pass...

Could we really see a peaceful world with benevolent leaders?

Are you ready to be a *working class hero*?

And how long till we get bored like past civilizations?

Once we reduce the bad and negative to negligible amounts can we really maintain the good and positive?

Well you know me, even while talking about all the shit that we wade through daily I remain ever the optimist.

Again a couple of the keys to this goal would be public access to all *true* historical records as well as transparency and accountability for all governments, corporations, and political organizations.

When I talk about *true* history, I am alluding to what really happened as apposed to the biased fictions written by the victors and survivors.

An exciting new area which scares the hell out of those currently running the show is hypnotic regression.

But let's quickly dismiss that as hocus pocus bullshit, right?

I'm sure like most processed consumers you have a number of reasons (or excuses) at the ready so that you can get back to those goals which you are working so hard towards.

Instead of FEMA emergency centres, we need deprogramming centres.

Like *A Clockwork Orange*, sometimes I get frustrated by just how ignorant most people are about their situation.

Sometimes it seems like just showing them the truth would help.

But really they have to want it in order for it to sink in.

Remember it is the ones who dress and act perfectly who are able to get away with the worst stuff.

The deterrents of our penal systems have only encouraged the liars and thieves to be more deceptive.

The harshness of our present, among other reasons, has contributed to the situation where most are just looking for their own little sanctuary.

But what if instead we rewire the now so that we can be open with all and share everything.

Consider that, seriously.

The Gods Of Our Universes

So another opportunity to share my personal experience.
But you're too busy posting selfies with your phone.
My perspective is invisible to you with your tunnel vision.
We are all separately the gods of our individual universes.
And as our lives continue, inevitably we will collide with another's
boundaries.
We've changed the outward appearances but our selfish bumper cars
continue to go in circles, as we can never leave the pay-per-play track.
I grew up watching Star Trek and reading Isaac Asimov but I still appear to
be the immovable centre around which the carousel revolves.
It looks pretty but goes nowhere.
I suppose I was hoping to meet someone with an engine that could blast us
off of this rock.
But it appears that all the engines are owned by the black project firms.
And I never got past the first interview.
That goddamn stumbling block called a conscience.
So many spooks, soldiers, suits, and shits have tried to convince me over
the years that their motives were noble.
But it appears that most (if not all) philanthropy is short-sighted and selfish.
Silly me I should just shut up, grab a brew, and watch the game.
You know, one of those rigged sporting events.

Every sport that you can legally (or illegally) bet on is rigged to some extent.

Anyway games are by definition amusing distractions which go nowhere. And once we get back to a time of peace and harmony on a global scale, then sure let's have some fun.

But for now in this double-think reality, I get the most pleasure from positively affecting my surroundings.

I would of course encourage others to be their best as well.

But knowledge is power and you can't build much with the dirt you are given if you don't know how to make bricks.

At some point in recent history certain knowledge and information has been hidden, stolen, distorted, etc.

WTF!?

This is the major common factor in all the rebellions of the past, present, and future.

Our sacred duty to pursue some peace of mind and return to a connection and participation in the eternal creation.

At the moment however humanity is like a child who has been told to sit down, be quiet, and watch cartoons.

If we are good, maybe we will get some milk and cookies.

TRS

Okay, so I recognize the efforts being made by many individuals and larger groups (Wikileaks, Anonymous, Noam Chomsky, etc).

We are learning to work together, more and more in the open.

We are getting closer to reaching a critical mass when the silent majority will feel safe to join in and explode these ideas onto the popular consciousness.

Now an important warning.

We have been trained in schools and by most of the popular propagandas to follow strong leaders.

And I realize that it has been hard-wired into our core beliefs to want to believe in benevolent gods and leaders.

But at the present time most of those who can get mainstream exposure aren't true or pure of heart.

So the movement must by necessity be tribal in nature and self-sufficient as well as cooperative with other like-minded groups.

Once again I am only sharing my thoughts and reflections.

I am not looking to be followed or quoted.

Just using the tools available to me and if it is helpful then I am encouraged.

On a personal note, usually when I go out and about I like to listen to my mp3 player playing what i consider to be cool music.

But today while I was at a coffee shop with my laptop, there was a period of about ten minutes where I had to pause the tunes.

And sitting next to me were a couple of under 18 girls who really disappointed me as a fellow human being.

Their discussion concerned them bragging about their recent successful lies and manipulations.

Which caused me to wonder what led them to be that way.

Was it a learned behaviour that they chose or were they made to feel that it was *cool* to be like that?

Though it is easy to be judgmental and elevate myself above their actions, in reality they are a prime demographic (to use the corporate expression) for this Transparent Revolution.

All of us as individuals will try to get our needs met by the tools that we have available to us.

So just think about the examples that the current generation is getting from war mongering leaders and corporations.

Or how about the completely detached from reality celebrities which command the attention of unprepared children with their absentee parents, both physically and emotionally.

You have to ask yourself why the majority of parents aren't warning their kids and teaching them what the reality of the situation is?

Are they just completely ignorant or are they simply so ashamed of their own role in the current fiasco?

Didn't they want this family which they are now a part of?

Are they simply doing the minimum that they feel is necessary?

Such a selfish society when even family members are keeping really crucial things from each other.

But with much of the picture viewed objectively we can see that to maintain the status quo "No good deed goes unpunished."

So you have to be crazy, weird, or just incredibly stubborn to continue to fight the good fight.

Most who know me would say I'm weird, I prefer the term crazy.

And I try to be stubborn but it is so tiring and I'm no Superman.

Which is why friends and compatriots are so precious.

As more truths continue to come out every day, many people are beginning to wake up to the importance of the struggle ahead of us.

And the more examples that they see of other like-minded people, the more of a chance exists that they will start to join in.

So it is very important that we be above reproach concerning our activities in and out of the movement.

Now that is a rather troublesome statement for many people.

I mean who has the right to tell you what to do, right?

Very quickly, I would say that we must regulate ourselves.

By that I mean that I should honestly look at myself and modify my behaviour as well as the things which I am consciously or unconsciously contributing to.

It is of course a constant struggle in the current environment.

The demonic (for lack of a better term) corporations at the top of our current economic hierarchy have what amounts to unlimited advertising budgets.

And all the metadata collected from our phones, social media, purchasing habits, and on and on and on...

Has given them incredible insight into what we will or won't do in most foreseeable scenarios.

Which of course makes it quite simple to steer us in whatever direction suits them.

Hypothetical Problem #1: The economy is going into recession.

* no worries *

Solution: Covertly fund a group of radical *freedom fighters* in a foreign country. Point them in a certain direction and then at the appropriate time (read when it is politically useful) condemn them and use the full force of propaganda to unleash the anger of the population who will fund the armed forces necessary to fight these new evil enemies. After all, nothing stimulates the economy like a *good* war.

Hypothetical Problem #2: The citizens are starting to wake up to important issues like the quality of the foods, medicines, and products available.

* no worries *

Solution: It is an election year, so empower some preposterous candidates who grab the headlines with their outrageous antics. Racism, homophobia, and other Nazi-like appeals to the *sheeple*. Now what do you know, most people don't seem to notice that other major countries have banned Monsanto GMO foods. And mainstream media sure isn't covering alternative medicine breakthroughs.

So back to reality, with that kind of counter intelligence available to the money machines (aka Wall Street, Military Industrial Intelligence Complex, etc), it almost seems like we need to create a parallel universe to move to while leaving the machines to continue their conquest of this space-time.

But alas they would just follow us through the portal like Terminators.

There simply doesn't appear to be, whoops hold on now...

That is one of the most effective deterrents available.

Blitz us with a constant and overwhelming show of power until we cower back into our caves and huddle around the campfires with our loved ones.

Nothing we can do about the big picture, right?

Always remember that it is just a human verses human struggle and all those weapons and armour that they use are because we completely outnumber them.

Also, we've been doing all the heavy lifting for quite some time now.

So if it was a fair fight, we would win.

It is definitely long past time for full scale rebellion.

But it really needs to be the final revolution of humanities wheel of misfortune.

So once again I will suggest that we need to be proactive rather than reactive.

We need to be thinking long-term but not so far down the road that we forget to act now.

No more one voice movements led by dictatorial megalomaniacs.

I see a quietly consistent struggle and if you listen really hard you might just hear the Transparent Revolution Soundtrack playing in the background.

Lest We Forget

Laughter is the best medicine.

Indeed it is the only conventional remedy of any worth in this momentous contrariety.

Yup, there I go making up words again.

But what the fuck, we the 99% are swimming in a solution of 99% bullshit.

And at the present time the only ones reading this little scribble are my friends, online seekers, and those poor bastards recruited by NSA and other members of the Alphabet Soup.

Which reminds me, when Ed Snowden came into the public view, the US government tried to block its employees from gaining access to any of the info either released by him or about him.

Best of luck to the lumbering bureaucracy.

Can you even believe in luck anymore?

We have been beaten, raped, poisoned, imprisoned, abandoned, hijacked, low-jacked, bastardized, smothered, isolated, moulded, fractured, blinded, overwhelmed, and so many many more past the point where even my supposedly expanded mind can't even imagine for lack of a point of reference.

In the midst of all this I am reminded of all the children who are being abused on so many levels.

When I was in high school, the news reported a story about my grade four teacher who was being convicted of sexually abusing students.

And over the years I have partied with many many victims (god I hate that word) of abuse.

What a cycle of despair we are riding.

So that even though I understand the need for escape that the alcohol and drugs provide, I must implore you all to try to find a way to kick those habits so that you can truly be free.

The only thing in life that we should be addicted to is love.

No, not infatuation, sex, etc.

Unconditional love is where it is at people.

I know many of us have had to run from those who claimed to love us but really didn't.

So now let's start again.

Remember those places which you dreamed of in your happy moments.

Write down those pieces of your puzzling future.

Build the dream but not the one sold to you in the mass propagandas where everything you need has a price tag attached $.

The real dreams are made of loving relationships with the families that you choose.
The picture that I have chosen for many years now is a future where if someone tries to get seriously mad to the point of violence, they are simply smiled at and given a big hug.
But of course that is just my naive perspective, right?
We are all capable of so much uniqueness and originality.
So let's all do what we wish either together or separately while still connected by the love that binds us.
That is a worthy goal in my opinion and some of our free time could be spent trying to find ways of getting from here to there.
So okay one step forward, but then my friend tells me about some (at this point I struggle to find the appropriate term and fail) motherfucker who went into a nightclub in Orlando with a fully automatic assault rifle...
And just like that all those reoccurring debates come back up.
Of course first and foremost we should pay respect to and mourn the human losses of this unimaginable tragedy.
But like driving past a car crash where everyone has the need to slow down and gawk, the majority of us get sucked into the various heated debates.
Gun control, improved security, mental illness, homophobia, suspicions of terrorism, various conspiracies, and on and on...
My mind drifts back to what I know about the origins of mass propaganda.
Nazis, business advertising, MK Ultra, etc.
So that even if a little positive idea like the one proposed above were to get out into the *real world*, it could all too easily be swept aside by mass media or swallowed up by the *justice system*.
From a purely objective viewpoint, this is a rather fascinating situation.
How do we bring sustainable peace to a world filled with guns and various weapons of mass destruction?
I mean obviously eliminating all the weapons would be the ideal choice.
But there are numerous seemingly insurmountable obstacles to this strategy.
Firstly any move to persuade most gun owners to hand over their weapons would be met with distrust as though this was a precursor to some sort of overthrow.
Also even with some miracle resulting in the elimination of all kinds of weapons, what would stop people from building more?
Anyone with an internet connection can find all the information necessary to create 99% of the currently available weapons.
So in my opinion it always comes back to reducing the reasons for countries to go to war, and for individuals to covet each others possessions, and all the other instances of murder.

In the same way that alcohol and drug addiction is only a symptom of the real problem, so weapons proliferation is a symptom of a profoundly sick civilization. Which of course we all know but most feel helpless to affect any change.

And as individuals that is mostly true.

Another major cause of this recent *dis-ease* is the global resource land grabs by various countries and corporations around the world.

You know the ones, oil, coal, gold, diamonds, rare cell phone elements, etc.

So long as there is no realistic oversight to keep these greedy bastards in check...

I think we can all see where this is headed.

But one other thing that I was reminded of about the Orlando shooting.

I am not interested in speculating about motivation or any other uncertainties in this situation and I certainly do not wish to make light of or distract from the seriousness of the events.

However one thing that I think it important to pay attention to is what the greedy, selfish, and other despicable people are getting up to while the rest of us are grieving.

History has shown time and again that those without a moral compass will take advantage of a national tragedy to get away with whatever they can.

And while it would be nice if those in charge were watching and being vigilant, unfortunately the ones with the largest contributors end up running the show.

As Roger Waters put it in his album Amused To Death, "Don't be afraid, it's only business."

It is ironic that a lot of money is made by the elite while they keep us in a constant state of *busy-ness*.

But just a reminder to our so-called *betters*.

This is a physical world with actions and reactions.

When you persecute us, you make us stronger.

And your actions are always revealed in time.

We do not forgive. We do not forget.

Rabbit Hole

When a crisis comes, we like to believe that we will all pull together and help each other.

I personally hope that I will have compassion and good judgment.

However Hollywood reality is a far cry from what we encounter down here in the trenches and it is rather sanitized and biased towards certain party lines.

This is the part of understanding our current *human nature* where most of us will begin to bicker endlessly about things like political parties, countries, religions, etc.

And these are the things that are constantly being reinforced and manipulated to keep us at odds with each other.

No I am not standing here judging you and I am not interested in going through all the various pros and cons of everyone's particular belief systems.

But here is an important and simple test, which is also why it has been used and abused so often.

Is your choice or action a pro or con for humanity?

Now there was a time in my youth when I genuinely believed in our leaders. I now realize that it was a combination of my being naive and them being good liars who were aided by great propaganda.

But to get back to the question of what is good for humanity, that is something which we do and should wrestle with on a daily basis.

I suppose what would be an improvement would be if our choices were closer to being 50% pro and 50% con with our morality helping to make the choice.

Once again there are those who will question, "What is good morality?", as though I am forcing them to be a certain way.

Personally my morality is to try and treat others the way which I hope others would treat me.

Of course I also live in a reality where I am by and large surrounded by those who only speak to me when they want something.

And when my trust is abused over and over...

Like I said before, we are kept in the mud wrestling each other.

And our collective belief systems are so fragmented and pulling us in so many different directions that we cancel out each others efforts.

Not much need for *Big Brother* to step in and swat us down, for the most part we are selfish little amoral pitbulls fighting over the GMO scraps which our masters have allotted us.

I stand by a statement that I made long ago, "We mock your answer to the problem only to get your attention. We are not going to steal your wallet or wreck your life. We know the stock market crash left you plenty of strife."

Let me reiterate part of the grand idea.

We are all here in this moment to find solutions to what ails each other, the planet, etc.

If you don't want to participate, at least get out of the way.

The time for countries invading one another to gain an advantage is over.

The time for drug addiction in all its forms is over.

The time for rape whether it be physical, spiritual, or emotional is over.

The time for greed to fill those never-ending holes is over.

The time for abusing humans, animals, and the environment is over.

The time for clinging to antiquated traditions is over.

This is now our time together, get over it!

We are, we create, and we see the people, places, and things that have been and will be necessary for a sustainable peaceful reality.

What are your true talents and desires that can be used and striven toward?

Those are some pretty exciting ideas and possibilities.

So let's make the effort to build a reality (home, city, planet, etc) which we can be proud of.

With the same attention to detail put into making a Hollywood film or a crowd funded video game.

No more disposable products designed with planned obsolescence in mind, filling up landfills.

No more public infrastructure projects given to political friends with no quality control or accountability.

No more elections for the most powerful positions in which we the 99% have to look the other way and pretend that we are not getting *royally fucked*.

No more entertainment/propaganda systems which spend a good deal of time on the one hand convincing us to fight for bullshit rights like the right to get drunk and stoned, while convincing us on the other hand that we don't have the right to know where our tax dollars are going.

No more suppression of free and or renewable energy sources and that includes the elimination and or disappearances of those advocating said energy sources.

No more bitching about immigrants while at the same time ignoring the reasons why they felt the need to leave their home countries (war, famine, genocide, religious persecution, etc).

Yup once again I have jumped down that disparaging rabbit hole called the really real world but I am no longer overwhelmed by the sheer magnitude of it all.

When you begin to see the interconnections and or those responsible and their techniques, tools, machinery, bureaucracies, etc...

It then becomes easier to mount at least the beginnings of a response.

Finally a real war for our generation.

It will be unique in its goals and objectives and also in the fact that it is being fought for the *right reasons* with *no collateral damage*.

Unrealistic

Collateral damage is one of those terms which gained widespread use by the military as a way to describe the killing and maiming of innocent civilians and allied troops without really saying so.

I believe that it is important to repeat the term *innocent civilians* as that is another term which has been used in a biased fashion.

When USA forces or their allies kill innocent civilians, it is reported in their home media as *collateral damage* as though they painstakingly went out of their way to avoid these regrettable incidents.

But alas, unfortunately those darned civilians got in the way at the last minute.

Of course when civilians get killed by our supposed enemies, they are called *innocent civilians*.

By now it should be apparent to anyone that when the numbers of *collateral damage* victims begin to reach into the millions, they aren't so much rarities as business as usual.

But what the fuck can we civilians do about this locally funded genocide and out-of-control global bullying?

That's a good question don't you think, considering that many many people have been protesting such things since at least the 60s and Vietnam?

But back then most civilians and military personnel alike genuinely believed the lies that their governments were telling them.

And in order to affect any sort of change, the protest movements of the time had to be very visible in their efforts and easily recognizable.

So it didn't take much for the military industrial complex lackeys to discredit, silence, and generally eliminate these efforts.

Fast forward to the present *state of affairs* and we have a completely different ball game.

Now we have a situation where the majority of the public and military personnel have a healthy distrust of their governments and military leaders.

The vocal unrest is growing both in the street and online.

So how is it that these bastards are still not only able to continue their barbaric actions but are actually able to increase their frequency and severity?

Really, I'm asking!

And I damn sure know that I am not the only one asking these questions.

I am personally aware of many of the answers but *knowledge is only the beginning of wisdom*.

And it seems like most of those who were inclined to actually take action in correction of these injustices have already been removed from the scene through various means (lies, entrapment, planting of evidence, disappearances, etc).

To the point now where all we seem to have left are a group of Facebook friends who have to think long and hard before they *like* anything that is considered too controversial and *weekend* protesters who will only participate up to a point.

If one were to graph the rights and freedoms of we the 99% over the past seventy years or so, the picture would be that of a bell curve with our present situation heading towards the bottom once again.

One thing that comes to mind again is the idea that even if you bandage up a couple of wounds, until you remove the underlying cause more will continue to emerge.

So even though many brave people have won some hard fought battles for our rights and freedoms in the past, because others didn't take up the torch and keep up the momentum we are seeing a resurgence of the oppressive beast that was never really slain but only wounded.

In previous statements that I have made, I have pointed out that this will be a generational struggle much like breaking the cycles of child abuse, rape, and racism.

We have in recent times exposed a good deal of previously hidden information which has definitely helped to paint a more complete picture of our situation.

But knowing that you are drowning doesn't automatically mean that you will spontaneously learn how to swim.

I have heard many people remark about our current situation (corruption, genocide, AIDS, etc), that if it were to truly get out of control then the citizens would rise up and overthrow the perpetrators.

And if we are to take the *approved* history books at face value and transport ourselves back in time a hundred years or so, that might be true.

However most of the important points in those books are massively distorted or even completely fabricated.

Like when we are told that a people's revolution happened in order to bring about freedom and liberty, but in reality the revolution was instigated and funded by some powerful bankers to oust a leader who wasn't being a good little puppet.

Maybe we all need a pair of sunglasses that will reveal the reality behind the illusions and a universal bullshit translator that will decode the truth from the persistent lies.

Not that it would help in all cases, like when we uncovered the Hillary Clinton emails exposing her lies and misdeeds only to have the law enforcement officials give her a free pass to run for commander and chief of the good old US of A.

Our new adventures into the world of reality and truth are a lot like exploring virtual reality for the first time.

Everything appears a bit fuzzier, the controls aren't at all intuitive, and it is only accessible in short doses resulting in massive headaches.

But it is amazing what you can get used to, right?

At this point I am probably mostly preaching to the choir, so to speak.

Most of us know the truth when we hear it and who we should truly consider as role models.

Wouldn't it be nice to have an entire generation of parents who were heroes to their kids for all the right reasons?

Not just for paying the bills and supplying them with the latest gadgets that *all the other kids have* but for helping to make their world a more just and humane place to live in.

In my lifetime, I haven't seen much of a shift away from many of the old prejudices. Sure there has been plenty of talk about how things should be and most people *act* civilized in public, but when they are alone with their friends then their true feelings come out.

It's pretty sad really.

Just because god is dead now for more and more people along with their false dogmas, doesn't mean that their humanity has to die along with it.

In my experience, the truest thing that I can tell you my friends is that we collectively manifest our reality.

So let's try something a little different this time.

Let's build a reality where our only god is love.

And instead of trying to envision mythical deities with invisible realms, let's once and for all expand and define the many faces of real love and set that as the goal for our collective manifestation.

Yup, there I go being un *real* istic again!

Rebellion

Race wars and other things we probably shouldn't do.

Sounds like a Woody Allen film but really in a world that has been massively mobilized for war since at least WW2 what are we supposed to do with all our tanks, missiles, war ships, and those millions of rounds of ammunition?

I recently read that someone had found a way to positively convert plastic into usable energy.

We should start a think tank aimed at finding peaceful and positive uses for all that death machinery.

But even if we eliminate the war toys then what do we do with the troops, generals, and dictators?

It seems to me that we are going to need a whole new army of councillors and a fleet of self help groups to transition the troops back into civilian life. I'm not joking either.

Let's take ~1/3 of the money currently spent on *defence* and put it towards retasking the war machines for peaceful use, another ~1/3 towards transitioning our soldiers into lives that they can be honoured to live, and the final ~1/3 on *little things* like education, housing, and health care.

How can we possibly do that, you exclaim?!

Well first off we need to wrestle for control of the decision making processes that lead us to war in the first place.

I mean what a vicious cycle that is.

For example, a lobbyist for a weapons manufacturer picks up the phone and calls some political big wig complaining that their sales have dropped and they need a new sale.

Then many calls later Obama and Putin are insulting each other on TV.

So let's brainstorm a way to prevent that inhumane corporate power play from ever happening again.

Checks and balances people.

Transparency and accountability with some decent people involved in the major decisions.

But that sounds like politics you say and it is becoming clearer every day how politics is like one big *secret society*.

In order to get to the point where a *person* in politics is given the power to decide which contracts get awarded to which companies that *person* has already gone through so many initiations and jumped through so many hoops that there really isn't much of a *person* left.

These days, the majority of the population don't even believe that it is possible to be a politician with integrity.

Really that should be a big red flag which causes the vast majority to look up and shake their heads saying, "What the fuck is going on?!"

But with a seriously integrated system incorporating surveys, questionnaires, and state-of-the-art propaganda, all of this disturbing behaviour is made palatable with late show punchlines and prime time comedy satire.

I mean come on now, we all seem to be too busy trying to pay our bills, cure our illnesses, and have fun to worry about the *small stuff* like our increasing enslavement.

So a new major focus that we seem to need is to be communicating our messages in ways which truly get the important points across and also reach as broad a *demographic* as possible.

Having an in depth conversation with a couple friends who already agree with us isn't a very good use of our time.

At some point each of us needs to decide that we are going to make a number of these issues a major priority in our lives.

There really isn't an example which we can follow for changing our future as we are in uncharted territory.

Being a better person than the norm and being open and honest about what we believe to be important and true is a good step in the right direction.

So much of our current common interaction is spent regurgitating the latest sensational antics of the politicians and A-list celebrities or claiming to be shocked and surprised by the latest mass shooting and/or *terrorist attack*.

It has been shown that certain musical styles can either increase or decrease a persons attention span and thus their potential for reasoning and deep thought.

So turn off the *radio* for a little while and really think about what I just said. While I personally respect the talents of Tupac and Marshall, hip hop music is one of those styles which reduces a person's attention span.

And don't get me started on what all those 30 second television advertisements have moulded us into.

Anyway that topic is an easy tangent to get sucked into.

So use technology for your own benefit but don't let it make you into a puppet.

Also, we are now in a transition stage for privacy as Snowden and Assange (among others) have shown us.

So let's organize the shit out of this Rebellion, but we need to be smarter than the average bear.

Recognize that the majority of people are with us so long as our intentions are clear.

Which is why the corporate media is trying so hard to bait the average citizen into emotional reactions on so many levels and why when we make a statement they will try to find any small negative issue to magnify and distract from our intended message.

So be vigilant, patient, and determined.

Free From The Yoke

So we are out and about.

We are living the dream.

And then something out of place catches our eye, so we stop and stare.

But we are busy people and surely someone else will find a solution to this problem.

Not us, we are busy people.

So now the question of the day:

When the Revolution begins, what are you as an individual prepared to do to help the Revolution?

So far everyone that I have asked lately has laughed it off saying something like, "I'm John Connor, I'll lead them." or, "I'll kill them all!"

Because in reality most people can't imagine it happening, let alone being a part of it.

We here in Can/America have only ever seen real dissent on TV or in the movies and that is usually over in about 2 hours.

Can you imagine what a protest lasting for only a week would do to most twenty-somethings?

Yup that means:

-no PlayStation.

-no alcohol/drugs.

-no decent sleep.

-no showers.

-irregular eating schedules.

-inconsistent medication intervals.

Sounds appealing right?

But really what do we have to be upset about anyway?

Well let's see...

Here's a small list off the top of my head:

-my water is polluted.

-my food is poisonous.

-my rent is crazy high.

-my wages are crazy low.

-my taxes are killing people in far away countries.

-my votes are pointless choices between whichever corporate puppet has told the best lies.

And on, and on...

So how do we know that our water and food is poisonous?

Well it won't be the government telling us, they would be on the hook for letting it happen.

But wait, people have been worried about this stuff for years now so there must be a test kit that we can purchase to test for bad stuff so that we can know that what we are ingesting is safe, right?

Not a fucking chance in hell!

The last thing that corporate North America wants is evidence that we are being fed poison by the shovelful.

That would leave them wide open to class-action law suits which would strip them of the filthy booty which they have accumulated from years of modern class warfare.

And by now most people are waking up to the fact that Monopoly isn't just a board game.

No matter what emotional plea or manipulation that you hear, the root of all this strife is the barbaric economic weapons which are unleashed in unrelenting barrages, generation after generation.

Sure with the new plastics and microchips it all looks pretty but really not much has changed since the Native Americans were swindled with some trinkets and empty promises.

Metropolis is code for open-air prison.

Democracy is code for advanced enslavement.

Freedom of speech is code for, "Tell us what you really feel so we can fuck you up!"

Can you remember one single public figure that you have idolized who didn't get shot or seriously sell us out?

Now a lot of haters out there are gonna say that I am advocating a violent revolution where we summarily try and execute those who have betrayed the public trust.

Not at all, "An eye for an eye leaves the whole world blind."

And, "In the land of the blind, the one eyed man (or woman) is king (or queen)."

But I digress.

Honestly there is a torture far worse than killing them anyway.

Simply take away their money and power and bring them down to our level.

No need for floggings or walks of shame, just for them to live out their lives as regular persons but with the additional weight that everyone which they encounter on the daily will know of their past.

Everyone deserves the opportunity to atone for their misdeeds.

It is our choices that define us.

On a personal note, I chose most of the dark paths that I went down in my life.

In some cases I am still feeling the negative impact of those choices.

Like Yoda said, "Once you start down the dark path, forever will it dominate your destiny."

Well I don't believe anyone is a lost cause.

And sure as shit most of us humans aren't perfect little angels of light.

It's all about choices and intentions.

The trick is not to lie to yourself.

I think that we could have a pretty cool little rock here if we were open and honest with each other.

Now lately there has been a lot of talk about police forces and armies.

But really when you trace back the origins of large armed police forces and militias, you will find that it was for the most part done to protect the rich from the poor.

Oh sure some people try to tell us how law and order has helped to civilize us.

I would argue that we have civilized ourselves in spite of most of those laws.

And we all know that the rich are *above the law*, so it isn't a situation where those laws have helped to make people more equal.

As for police brutality and genocidal armed forces, if they were actually doing things that weren't being sanctioned by the elite, then you can be damned sure that orders would have come down from on high and that behaviour would have stopped.

But with people like Clinton and Trump as leaders in this craziness, I suppose these events are a predictable however tragic result.

As always my friends I am not simply cataloguing our misery here but raising issues which I hope that we can discuss in a proactive fashion.

Knowledge is power, especially if it is input for a dynamic system with unlimited potential.

That sounds like a good definition of humanity to me.

But like they say about computers, garbage in garbage out.

Which is precisely why we are taught useless and fraudulent info in our education systems.

If the powers that be wanted a crop of geniuses and nurturers, then that's what we would see.

But what they really want are slaves with just enough intelligence to do their jobs and lifespans just long enough to be productive.

They have gotten pretty good at managing these factors.

But occasionally some people start to figure things out and then others see their example and start to wake up.

And if they aren't careful those damned slaves will be demanding civil rights and an environment free from pollution.

We silly bastards, don't we realize that we are just pets with invisible leashes.

Time for a false flag op to circumvent what little freedom we do have.

There that's better, now we are too busy fighting pointless wars and worried about invisible terrorists for us to mount any useful challenge to their monopoly.

What the hell did we hope to achieve anyway, we have been told that we are up against a *god* who can strike down towers of Babel, turn people to salt, and drown us with a flood just to name the greatest hits.

Have you ever noticed that there aren't any myths or stories about a group of determined citizens freeing themselves from the yoke of a tyrannical *godlike* overlord?

Sounds to me like a story that needs to be written.

You want to play?

How About You

Well then what would you like to talk about?
Okay let's discuss how you love to walk the beach on a breezy day.
Or how about the fact that you can't stop smiling when you talk about the
cute guy that you met rock climbing?
Maybe we should have a good laugh about how wasted you got last night.
Or that guy playing Pokemon on the subway tracks was hilarious of course.
Right then, time to get back to our servitude.
It was a good thing that we didn't run out of happy shiny things to say.
Then we may have discovered that you were too shallow and I was too
deep.
But really we're just two bumper cars passing on the concrete of this
congested containment.
At this point it is a toss-up whether the next major crisis will be a martial
law crackdown or a disorganized rebellion.
Either way the Ghostbusters can't help us and Pokemon has been hacked.
Do you dare to take a side or just give up after pondering the choices during
a commercial break for The Real Housewives of *who gives a fuck*?
Yup it's safer that way alright.
No worries, with all the neurotoxins and addiction rollercoasters from what
you inhale and ingest daily, you probably won't even notice what you are
missing.
Yes I am somewhat bitter today.
I don't have any children of my own yet but I suppose this is a lot like the
frustration that many parents feel while watching their kids repeating the
same mistakes which they made in their youth.
At one of my first jobs, a manager told me that people are like cattle.
And that if you set up a rope line, they will line up on their own.
I have seen that demonstrated numerous times over the years, mostly in
common everyday situations.
However it also plays out in some pretty serious scenarios.
Most people would like to believe that these types of tragedies are just
dreamed up for the movies.
But like I have said before, art is simply an interpretive reflection of our
reality.

And as always the worst atrocities are perpetrated at a distance by our economic overlords.

I'm sure in some far removed perspective like a Star Trek Federation council meeting, our plight would be considered a minor blip only mentioned in passing

I suppose in time people will reminisce about our era like we speak of the dark ages, using vague references and ignorant indifference.

The long string of atrocities by our various leaders will be omitted in the interest of brevity.

So why do *we* try so hard as individuals to make these little differences? That is a really important question and unique for everyone involved, although I personally will keep those reasons to myself.

Which in my case is partially because I would rather not give The Machine more ammunition for its control system.

After all propaganda is all about modifying people's thoughts and behaviours, which is easier to do if you know what causes those thoughts and behaviours.

The real point is that we have made the choice to do our part to improve our situation.

Too many people these days *improve their situation* in true capitalistic fashion by taking from their friends and co-workers in order to benefit themselves.

But what I am talking about when I refer to *our* situation is the global village that we collectively share.

So we really need to gather enough info to think globally and act locally for the long and short-term benefit of the 99%.

Wouldn't it be nice to speak of *we the 100%*, like we *all* just missed something and need to pull up our socks and work together towards a better future for everyone.

But so long as we, for the most part, get our big picture perspective from sources owned and operated by those who have an interest in keeping us ignorant about many of the crucial situations happening globally...

Nope there's no Santa Claus, Easter Bunny, or people in financially lucrative positions who aren't bought and sold by the cartels.

And I am not just talking about the *drug cartels* either.

There are more types of cartels than Skittles flavors.

Also just a reminder that there are at least three major political/economic ideologies which are in a perpetual state of war with each other.

In much the same way that George Orwell (Eric Blair) had three rotating enemies in his book 1984.

The three largest are the modern equivalents of the Russian Communists, German Nazis, and American Capitalists.

Of course, for the most part, we can see the actions of the KGB and CIA but most people are either unaware or have forgotten about the hidden hand which guides and finances groups like ISIS.

Which makes things really confusing by design and I have been wrong in the past attributing ISIS growth to US negligence, at least in its entirety.

When WW2 ended many of the Nazis scurried off to various places.

And most people who have cared to look are aware that many of the most *useful* Nazis who were found in and around Germany after the war were taken by the Americans and Russians.

But of course there were many who weren't accounted for.

We like to believe that any of the ones who escaped lived out the rest of their lives in fearful hiding.

But really there were a number of groups and regimes who were more than happy to give them shelter and accept some of the Nazi booty.

Many of us have heard recently that the FBI knew that Hitler was alive after the war.

But in reality the figure heads of the Nazi party weren't really the powers of the underlying organization.

They were by and large *tools* to achieve certain aims of which the recent European Union was one.

Now going on more than 70 years since war's end, who really knows what an updated list of tools and goals would look like?

And I think that it is really important to make people aware that many of the *resistance* movements that we see causing trouble recently aren't necessarily wholesome grass roots movements or the product of American and Russian foreign policy gone awry.

Also when those at the perceived top of the global power pyramid claim that there is no organized collusion of the major economic instruments (stock exchanges, central banks, multinational corporations, etc) it is so laughable that I almost feel it shouldn't need to be said.

But such is the strength of certain national propaganda machines that their brainwashed citizens are left so completely lacking in facts that they form patterns of probability based on staggeringly deficient data.

Okay then, let's *re form* our ideas for global unity taking into account this *new* information.

Let's start with the two *superpowers* of Russia and USA.

What if we eliminate the tools that are used on a daily basis to pit these long-time rivals against each other?

And what if we are able to effectively apply transparency and accountability to the worlds of politics, economics, health, education, etc?

Yes I know it is probably time to wake up from this nice little daydream, right?

But is this really a pointless pursuit which will ultimately end in dismal failure?

Or is it possible that with enough people away from their video games, alcohol/drugs, sporting events, divisive politics, under-payed employment, etc...

Is it really possible that with enough popular support and a true understanding of the situation we could come to an above-board agreement with these groups who have broken away from the rest of us?

It appears to me with my limited understanding that there is already some interaction between them and some of our higher level officials.

But to some extent they seem to have us *by the balls*, so to speak.

This is where the discussion veers off the road of commonly accepted reality.

In 1952 there were overwhelming reports of UFOs in Washington DC, commonly referred to as the *Washington UFO flap*.

And in 1947 there was a US Navy mission to the Antarctic entitled *Operation Highjump* in which those troops were repelled by a superior force.

Whether that repelling force was due to numbers or technology is debatable.

And over the years there has been overwhelming evidence of the presence of UFOs around the world.

Now the spin-doctors and propagandists have done a good job of minimizing and discrediting these facts and experiences.

And I will certainly agree that there is a large percentage of the population who are over/self medicated, which can lead to paranoia and hallucinations. But most rational people capable of critical thinking come to the same conclusions, that there is simply far too much going on to be easily dismissed as fantasy.

So once we jump that hurdle of disbelief, the only really important question remaining is who is responsible for these technologies and encounters?

And when we eliminate the fantasies of alien invasions and time travellers, then what do we have left?

How about a heavily funded breakaway group with their own agenda and research unhampered by little things like moral safeguards.

I mean if the founding members were Nazis and the like, then what does that say about their ruthlessness?

Think about it, we here in Can/America get worried about groups like CIA and NSA getting out of control.

And those are groups with some *limited oversight*, just consider what 70 plus years of unchecked research and experimentation might amount to.

I think even science fiction writers could have some trouble imagining that one.

Now of course those who remember what happened in the lead up to WW2 realize that a string of appeasements is simply delaying the inevitable.

Also another point to consider is the idea that nothing is more fearful for human beings than *the unknown*.

So it all may just be a big misunderstanding stemming from a lack of information.

But if so then maybe they could explain why so much money and effort is put into these technologies instead of helpful little areas like education, healthcare, housing, etc?

That is really the biggest stumbling block to the *don't worry, be happy* ideology.

If things are really progressing along nicely then why are so many innocent people getting slaughtered on a daily basis?

Someone certainly has some explaining to do.

I think most of us would certainly make the time to have a sit down for some truth.

I would definitely volunteer in any capacity to help that happen, how about you?

Nothing To Lose

Right then, our network has been established.

We put out a call for new recruits and the replies have been overwhelming.

Our goals have been debated and debated and finally a consensus has been achieved.

We have agreed to major changes for a wide variety of key areas which will quickly facilitate relief for a large percentage of those among the 99% who are suffering the most at the present time.

Many of those at the higher end of the power pyramid have pledged their assistance in mediating the transitions of potentially inflammatory situations.

A high percentage of civil servants are either actively participating or have agreed to monitor and report on suspicious government activity.

The same can be said for many of those employed in the military and corporate sectors.

But do we have enough of the key players on board to ward off the many potential blood baths?

And how about the numerous economic upheavals which are absolutely inevitable in the long transition?

This is actually the one aspect of which I am the least concerned.

Money has ruled our planet for a while now and once we take greed out of the equation we have a pretty good idea of how to make economics work for us.

I would say at the moment that I am most concerned with the racial and religious unrest that is so close to the surface these days.

Those who have been indoctrinated into a belief that they are better than someone else because of their faith or skin colour will need time to let go of their prejudices.

And an adjoining issue will be those who have been or feel that they have been wronged by another *race* or religion.

Of course more and more people are waking up to the idea that it has never been shown that skin colour has any bearing on someone's abilities or potential.

And as far as I know no one has ever proven that *god* has a specific set of rules which we are supposed to follow.

My joke for a while now has been that if the *big* guy or gal did have a list of absolute commandments then they would have been genetically tattooed onto our bodies in the womb.

So anyway I am personally putting out a call to all *thugs* whether they are currently involved in law breaking or enforcement.

I recognize that most of you had good reasons for your career choices. However *the times they are a changin'*, and there will certainly be good uses for your particular skill sets in helping to maintain a common respect for one and all during these times of potential chaos.

For too long now we have all had so many various individual goals that were at odds with each other in so many ways that it would probably be impossible for all our computers networked together to unravel and sort out. And no this is not the product of human nature or fate, we have been collectively played off against each other in classic Machiavellian style. Because when you have a post Babel type civilization with multitudinous languages, faiths, nationalities, cultures, etc...

Then divide and conquer is quite an easy and effective strategy for control. Which is a major reason why our current governing systems with Monarchs, Presidents, Prime Ministers, and the like are all *prime* targets for corruption.

It's a simple equation really, it takes less time and money to buy one politician than to try and control the ideals of an entire population.

We've all seen this play out in many scenarios over the years and generally the situation goes like this:

For one reason or other there is an ending of leadership in a certain country, so many people begin to challenge for the *throne*.

And so long as the victor is willing to play ball with the *powers that be* whether they be multinational corporations, powerful foreign governments, or the internal elites then it will be business as usual.

However, and especially in recent years with increased internet availability, there is a greater likelihood of a growing unrest in the majority of the poorest citizens.

So some poor bastard is convinced that he or she should run for office to help fix the corruption.

And should they win the election then they are quickly made aware of the expectations of the *real* ruling powers in the country.

This is not usually a single entity but rather a combination of corporations, cartels, militaries (either foreign or domestic), etc.

And soon they will be faced with the big question of how far they are willing to go to protect their citizens from the negative effects of corruption in their country.

David and Goliath doesn't even come close to describing the overwhelming odds facing these patriots who will either lose their lives or their souls.

The assholes running *the show* have gotten really good at persuading these sacrificial lambs to play along.

But still the occasional *crazy* leader attempts to defy the odds and is eventually eliminated.

I am sure that I don't need to give a list of the numerous recent examples as I am only restating what we all know but have learned to live with.

How about you, are you happy?

Are you looking forward to the conversation with your children about how you did nothing to make their world a more peaceful and loving place?

In fact all that we have really done lately is learn which drugs to take which will numb the pain but leave us able to continue our enslavement with a smile.

We are like prisoners living in an invisible prison who spend their lives learning to live within the constraints of their incarceration.

Oh sure we all believe that we are doing our best but that is no longer good enough.

One popular idea recently is that we should just *not enlist* in the armed forces as though reducing the number of soldiers would somehow stop the perpetual conflicts being waged globally.

Not realizing that with the availability of automated killing machines on the rise (drones, etc.), all that would happen is that there would be a slick ad campaign showing us how compassionate our leaders are and how they have *heard the cries* of the fallen soldier's families and are now asking for increased funding and more automated weapons.

Anyway I could spend all day on the countless ways that humanity has been, is currently, and may be totally screwed in the future.

But I think we are passed needing to be convinced of such things, so let's get back to our individual roles in the much needed Rebellion.

I truly believe that one really important thing to consider is the idea of wiping the slate clean for past offences (for the most part).

Of course that doesn't mean putting pedophiles in charge of kindergarten or blatantly absurd things like that.

But grudges like Russians and Americans refusing to work together or Muslims with Jews or Christians, etc.

Also financial debts should either be completely eliminated or at least reduced to easily manageable limits.

Then of course there is the out of control greed by many, such as couples who are living in mansions while large families struggle to live in inadequately small shacks.

We need to prioritize in favour of love, peace, equality, etc.

There are so many things which could be fixed if we eliminate the need to turn a profit or the financial incentives of supply and demand manipulations.

Now many of the needed initial changes will cause many of the skeptics to claim that what we are proposing is similar to Communism or something else which has been demonized in the past.

But that is simply not a fair comparison as many of those who proposed some of these same ideas were doing so under false pretenses.

They were claiming to be for the people when in fact they were just telling the people what they wanted to hear in order to get into power.

And then once in power they progressively eliminated all of these people-friendly programs.

While what we are proposing here is a system with ironclad checks and balances.

Really the only ones with something to lose are the 1%, so what are we waiting for?

Believe That

Quite obviously the only ones still reading this insane train of thought are my fellow lunatics.

So I have a new idea for you all, are you ready for some clarity and prolonged periods of sanity?

Okay then let's start with our own personal health shall we.

Instead of simply protesting and bitching about how bad our foods and consumer products are, why not set some positive examples for others to follow.

Talk is cheap and everyone has an opinion but revolutions can't run on bitchin' opinions.

So off the top of my head, here is my current list of personal boycotts.

No more:

-Toothpaste or mouthwash with fluoride.

-Coffee, cola, chocolate, or other *foods* with caffeine.

-Soda pop, candies or other *foods* with glucose-fructose, corn syrup, or chemical sweeteners.

-Drugs of all kinds including: Pot, Hash, Coke, Mushrooms, E, etc.

-Alcoholic beverages.

-Tobacco products including cigars.

-Personally I haven't been diagnosed with any physical or psychological illnesses so I take only Tylenol when I have a bad headache.

-Also without all of the other crap coursing through my system, when I am sick I simply drink lots of fluids and maybe eat some oranges or grapefruits. But no cough medicine etc.

Okay, so that is a pretty comprehensive list.

I believe that anyone who follows those recommendations for a month will see an immediate benefit.

And after six months to a year they won't want to go back to poisoning themselves daily.

As far as benefits go, the ability to concentrate, to think deeply about complex issues, and an improved long-term memory are huge.

Also more physical stamina, strength, and longer life expectancy.

Of course there will be numerous withdrawal symptoms especially from caffeine, sugar, tobacco, and alcohol.

Which if you really think about it objectively is the reason why we have continued to do these things despite the overwhelming evidence of their negative effects.

It is really an intellectual domino effect when we allow ourselves to become a slave to these negative habits.

For example, let's say you start drinking alcohol regularly when you go out with your friends.

As that goes, eventually you overdo it and you begin to drink coffee regularly on the following mornings.

So now there are two things that you can't live without.

And of course when you drink too much there are a whole host of things that you might try for the first time during your state of inebriated lower inhibitions.

For example there's someone with a cigarette or perhaps a joint and you wonder what you're missing out on there.

What the fuck, you're already drunk right?

Then you wake up the next morning with a half pack of Marlboros or a couple joints.

No worries you can stop anytime, right?

Not bloody likely!

So now you are in a cycle of despair because you are now addicted to a number of things which are actually physically and psychologically causing you harm.

Which actually greatly reduces your ability to enjoy life's real pleasures and also physically impedes your capabilities as a human being.

And in large part you are in this predicament simply because you wanted to fit in and be *normal*.

In hindsight you can see that those people who seemed so cool were actually lost themselves.

And all those *cool* people smoking cigarettes or weed and drinking alcohol in the movies and on TV were fictional characters payed for by the Liquor Industry, Big Tobacco, and various Drug Cartels.

Welcome to the New World Order.

So our generation is now in a situation where we have given up one set of constraints for another.

We have shaken off many of the old religious dogmas.

We have fought for the rights of women, minorities, children, disabled people, the elderly, etc.

But while we were fighting for these issues, the bankster elite were stealing our rights to privacy, building their very own enforcement system, poisoning our food, water, and airwaves, etc.

Kind of like in chess when you focus on one small piece such as a bishop, meanwhile your king is being surrounded.

So we naively think that we have made some major gains but with these other new *systems* in place all this *progress* can be easily taken away for *reasons of national security*, etc.

Smoke and mirrors, they tell us what we want to hear meanwhile our global enslavement is planned dozens of moves ahead.

But only if we allow ourselves to be controlled, mislead, abused, poisoned, ignored, or disappeared.

"How can we possibly fight back?", you ask.

Well for starters we as a society need to stop allowing our *minds* to be bought, sold, and controlled.

I mean it isn't as if those running the show are actually more intelligent or creative than the rest of us.

They are ultimately just another cartel of drug dealers but with the exception that they have every drug you can imagine.

Do you want wealth, sex, power, joy, experience, toys, family, security, forgiveness, knowledge, etc?

No problem just sign away your soul on this piece of paper and remember to constantly live your life in fear of losing everything.

And always give us the best parts of yourself or you will end up being one of those tragic *losers* that we see on the news everyday.

You know, one of those poor bastards who are shot by the police for no apparent reason.

Or the ones who have their 15 minutes of fame from developing a new power source but then decide to commit suicide after it turns out that they lied and their invention never actually worked, and a nice oil company bought the patent just to be helpful.

Or a naive whistleblower who imagined that their particular revelation would usher in a new reality but who are then arrested for being in breach of trust from some fine print in their employment agreement.

Then while in prison they are put on suicide watch for unexplained reasons and are never able to get a moment's peace or a good night's sleep again.

And the list continues...

But don't worry about that, here's some idiot celebrities doing some outrageous shit.

Or how about that crazy weather lately?

And don't forget that WW3 could start any moment, so why worry about personal health and sanity?

Let's have an end of the world party every day for the rest of our lives.

Fuck that!

I remember when I was a child, I was living in the moment and constantly amazed.

Nowadays I wake up and suit up with various types of armour depending on the day.

I suppose at some point I decided to be a warrior in the age old battle of dark versus light.

Honestly though it wasn't my original intention.

I grew up kinda naive and really believed that there was more of us out here.

Fuckin' smoke and mirrors and by the time I recognized how deep down the rabbit hole I was, there was only one choice left.

Live free or die trying.

And now there is a growing global movement but here's the big catch.

We were collectively impotent for so long that the fight will be exponentially harder.

Don't worry I'm not giving up and neither should you.

But believing that you can fight back part-time or on the weekends is simply a waste of time.

Like a scene in Apocalypse Now, once you get out of the boat you have to be prepared to go all the way.

Now don't get all stressed out and think this is some sort of stupid-ass suicide mission or something like that.

Just get serious is all.

And I am sorry about getting a bit spiritual here but some of us made our choice to do our bit to help before we were born.

So if you aren't gonna join in then at least get out of the way and stop funding our adversaries.

I know that our free time is precious these days, so try focusing on health and quality whenever possible.

But it is no good to run off into the bush and try to ride out whatever troubles are coming.

My current perspective is that we should be a positive influence in whatever situation we find ourselves.

There are many systems which can be changed from the inside.

Of course not banking, arms manufacturing, politics, religion, etc.

But education, health, agriculture, architecture, air and water quality, transportation, etc can be eventually overwhelmed by positive internal influence.

So we can draw on our collective experience from at least a few decades of various types of protests.

We should be able to quite accurately predict which of our fights have a chance of succeeding.

And if we are able to organize on a larger scale, we should be able to increase our chances even more.

For too long now we have been doing short-sighted feel good protests which don't really change much.

And the mass public has gotten used to seeing us out there bitching about our *cause of the week*.

To them we are just more poor people begging for help out of a situation that we have apparently brought upon ourselves.

Certainly there are times to be human, happy, kind, loving, etc.

But we have been hiding from the tough choices of our species.

This is the part usually where someone would point out that we have been *turned into sheep*, brainwashed, etc.

Suffice it to say, "When I was a child, I spake as a child..."

But when you are raised in a war zone, you can't stay a child for very long.

It is time to get past the suspension of disbelief.

Dig deep inside of yourself first and figure out who you really are.

Not what you have been moulded into but the true spirit that is free to dream in the night.

Then build from that and be true to yourself.

We are no longer outnumbered freaks, we are the norm.

Sure most of us are timid and unsure of our first steps, like a child learning to walk.

But we were truly born for this shit.

Believe that!

Steroid Nazis From Argentina

We are not what we thought.

They are not what we have been taught.

It is all, that's all.

But really it isn't like most people give a shit.

Most *consumer drones* are just a collection of the products which they have settled for.

Our civilization is presently one big *virtual* reality show.

There really isn't much natural interaction happening.

Which is okay because we have been taught that nature is a dangerous bastard, right?

But products from our *trusted* corporate sponsors are much better, just ask that unnamed actor with the cool voice in the commercial.

All the online and telephone surveys combined with NSA (and others) metadata and all the other consumer data gathered and cross-indexed has given a pretty complete picture of what the average citizen will settle for over the span of their conveniently truncated lives.

When you really stop and realize that the majority of our daily choices are similar to choosing between three corrupt politicians, what does that tell you about the nature of your *reality*?

Most people settle for a culturally acceptable marriage partner and if they are able to have kids then they spend the rest of their lives working their asses off in order to buy more *products* to build their children out of.

But surely if we give our kids all the things we never had then their lives will be better, right?

Possibly but not likely.

You see our environment has for the most part been made safer but only from most people's perceptions.

It is a lot like believing what you see on TV.

First of all, the poisons in the water and the foods that we ingest daily aren't easily identifiable.

And there are various forms of radiations which are growing stronger every year.

Don't get me wrong I don't believe that things are past the point of no return.

But it will require an army of healthy individuals in mind, body, and spirit working together with transparency and cooperation to begin to make the first steps in the right direction.

What we don't need are a bunch of plain vanilla citizens produced by an industrial education system designed to supply an inhumane system with lever pullers and button pushers.

Our greatest assets as human beings are our creativity, adaptability, resilience, etc.

But when we send our children to various institutions for at least twelve years of the best parts of their lives with a gun to their heads forcing them to repeat, conform, and modify the very essence of who they are...

Well then are their lives really any better than ours were?

This is usually where we all want to blame someone else for *failing our kids*.

But ultimately the buck stops with the parents and they need to own that shit.

I do believe that most parents want their kids to be happy but wishing for something doesn't necessarily make it happen.

I could go on for a while about what I believe to be the best way to educate the youngsters.

But simply put, the main focus of change should be the removal of forced conflict.

They are constantly being placed in situations where they are in conflict with their classmates, which will eventually translate to conflict outside of the classroom and ultimately global chaos.

But we certainly don't see that in the real world, right?

WTF?!

Like I have said many times in the past after hearing it first from George Carlin, the education systems are producing what they have been programmed to produce.

We as a world population need to decide on some important major changes.

It really won't be as impossible as the propagandas continually suggest.

As always the main first step is to open up reliable friendly communication between all the people involved, which in this case is the entire population of the planet.

And all people need representatives who truly have their best interest at heart.

That really is the most crucial aspect of this *Utopian fantasy*.

So long as we have a group of two-faced liars controlling the military arsenals of the largest players on the planet then the entire planet will be living their lives in fear.

I believe that is where transparency comes in.

Because the ultimate example of where fear has lead us was the weapons proliferation of the cold war.

The Americans were led to believe that the Russians were far stronger militarily than they actually were.

So they built a huge stockpile of weapons and recruited an unnecessarily large number of troops.

Which in turn forced Russia to try to keep pace and ultimately caused their economy to collapse.

Meanwhile the USA became completely dependent on and addicted to its global war machine which was itself addicted to oil.

So when Russia finally collapsed and seeing as they were one of the two final superpowers, then more and more of the worlds problems became resolved using military means led by America.

And now we are here X.

But getting back to our *education* systems, the types of morality and conflict resolutions that we instill in the younger generations will ultimately translate into global politics.

The student war demonstrations of the 60s were viewed as warnings that were heeded by the military industrial intelligence complex.

Too much free thought, unity, and rebellion was a major threat to their power and profits.

And if you think that the standardized testing for students didn't have questions designed to identify *potential troublemakers*, guess again.

Once again let me state for the record that I am not accusing all government employees of conspiring against their fellow citizens.

With compartmentalization only a few people need to be privy to the real bottom line agendas.

And these techniques are being further refined every day.

Obviously a couple of perfect examples are 9/11 in the USA and 7/7 in Britain.

It has taken many years just to uncover the facts of these events.

Then the evidence had to be presented to the public through various means by mostly amateur enthusiasts with their own money.

All the while being ridiculed and *confidently* debunked by *experts* largely in the pockets of big business.

But finally the truth has been accepted by a majority of the population only to become popular knowledge *without any consequences* for those involved.

Kind of like when the FBI finally admitted that they knew Hitler had survived the war.

But we never heard of any consequences for this massive deception either.

Which unfortunately is an all too common situation which we have been conditioned to accept and actually expect.

These days the only people being punished by *law enforcement* are the poor and the truth tellers.

Just look at the number of innocent people being assaulted daily by the police in America.

Or how about the persecution of honest journalists and whistleblowers?

And look what is happening to the people who helped facilitate the exposure of corruption in the American Democratic party?

That was the sort of shit that we were raised to believe we should send troops to another country to prevent, wasn't it?

Wow, the hypocrisy is boggling!

So now we sit around with our families and friends waiting for better alternatives to magically appear.

Well here's a clue, *the revolution will not be televised* and it's not on Craigslist either.

At this point I am not gonna stand in judgment of what you are all individually doing with your time.

But really if your idea of a daily routine is something like:

Go to work or school, work your ass off, and then spend the little money that you have left over drinking and getting high before going to bed, rinse and repeat.

Then I really don't want to hear your bitching, respect is earned in this game.

Channel that energy into long-term growth with like-minded others.

The achievements will then start to multiply exponentially.

It has been proven over and over, which is why there are certain issues and organizational patterns which aren't expanded upon in mainstream media.

The only groups that I can think of which truly have decent off-grid organizational structure are the cartels and rogue black ops.

But in order to understand their structures to their fullest extent, you would have to have been in so deep that you would never get out, let alone contribute to a blockbuster movie script or a best-selling novel.

And what it really comes down to is *complete soul shattering corruption*.

Imagine Nazis who were never actually human to begin with, then you have a better understanding of the mindset.

Kind of like the British royal family or some other self-entitled inbred closed-loop power systems.

When a *person* grows up completely detached from a so-called regular life and are then put out to the commoners as someone who can help but is in fact just another part of the enslavement control system with no power to enact any real changes...

I would empathize with their plight and say that their situation has to suck but really they don't appear to have much in the way of emotions at all.

Anyway that is what we are in the middle of for this current miserable human drama.

We in this rebellion subculture would like to believe that simply exposing the fascists for who they truly are will be enough to sway public momentum.

But the more that I learn about the true history of this global enslavement, the more I see the reoccurring cycles of exposure, rebellion, suppression, annihilation, naivety, revelation, exposure, rebellion...

The only things that never actually change in this situation are the true powers behind our so-called leaders which we call kings, presidents, queens, prime ministers, etc.

This is where it all starts to sound a bit crazy, like the rest was 100% sane. "Who are the overlords of these dimensions which we inhabit?", you might ask.

Well if I had specific info about the individuals and groups acting in concert with each other globally, then I am quite certain that I wouldn't be able to write this little scribble for much longer.

Ya I know it sounds a whole lot paranoid.

I make no apologies for following the clues and trying to expose the truth.

I know it sounds pretty cliche but what would you be willing to give up in the short-term in order to gain your freedom in the long-term?

Personally I have risked sanity, financial security, physical health, and incarceration.

But really most of that was the byproduct of being a naive stubborn truth seeker.

If someone had shown me the trials and tribulations that I would go through, I probably would have chosen something easier to be obsessed with.

But there is also the idea that we all choose the life we lead before we are born.

So in that case I would be braver than I thought.

And really any of us alive today deserve a little respect just for showing up.

Also it is a tremendous opportunity for so many reasons.

We can go in any direction we want from here, regress or progress, devil or saint, motionless or active.

And it is far more complicated than even combining all the books, songs, and films together would suggest.

They say that Earth is a school and mostly we are here to learn how to live with these crazy emotions.

To run the gambit between fear and love while not burning down the place in the process.

There is no basic formula for success, truth.

Apathy Olympics

Okay let's change gears a little bit here and examine the apathy which is so abundant these days.

There are the overly religious who have been trained to believe that everything is going according to some plan, so don't worry.

There are the overly cynical who have trained themselves to believe that there is in fact no plan, so it's everyone for themselves.

There are the overwhelmed whom life has beaten into submission, so they keep their heads down.

There are the ordinary ignorant who don't really have an opinion, so they just keep on keepin' on.

And of course there are also many many more variations of *minority* opinions, so no nobody really cares.

But there are also a number of groups *in the know*.

These are the ones who have had their way for far too long.

They aren't allowed to be directly portrayed in the mass media (films, books, TV, etc.).

They have been running a really sinister show with no signs of any respect for our *basic humanity*.

And when I attempt to make allowances for the things that I don't yet comprehend.

Or look for signs that we could possibly be coming out of this nose dive which has sent us plummeting towards the ground for many years now.

Well I gotta say that I haven't seen shit!

Basically here is what is going on with regards to us lowly peasants...

Life on Earth is currently in a period of darkness for various reasons.

The *educated* and *advanced* are only shown the bigger picture once they have proven their unwavering allegiance to the darkness.

And we have seen examples of what happens to the occasional *elitest* who unwittingly grows a conscience.

Car accidents, drug overdoses, suicides, insider trading convictions, drunk driving, etc.

Meanwhile the *average* citizen is robbed of any ideas regarding humanitarian aspirations by the many prevalent tools of mass mind control.

This is where their emotions are played upon like musical instruments.

They are trained like dogs and cats to only care about themselves and their families.

Sure there are some groups off in the *untouched wilderness* who have great relationships with each other and their environment.

But they aren't an economic, political, or military threat to the ruling powers of the country, planet, solar system, etc.

So for the time being they are left alone.

I recently watched *Snowden*, the new Oliver Stone film.

It is a must see for a number of reasons but there were a couple of things about my theatre experience which were disappointing.

Like I have said before I live in Vancouver, British Columbia.

And this show wasn't even given top billing in its opening week.

Also, I could tell from most people's reactions in the theatre that almost all the material was new to them.

I suppose most people hadn't seen *Citizenfour*, which is also quite disappointing.

So I guess what really annoys me is that so many people remain wilfully ignorant about these crucial facts of life.

Don't worry though, I'm not giving up on you guys.

I know that we all have insecurities, baggage, and responsibilities which keep us busy.

And we have been sold proprietary hardware like PlayStations which only give us a narrow vision of reality.

Amused To Death indeed.

Keep in mind that all TV shows, films, and video games which are given access to military and/or *intelligence* agencies for *authenticity* have agreed to only portray those various organizations in a favourable light.

And don't get me started on the product placement fictions which make all our heroes into chain-smoking, hard-drinking, etc.

Meanwhile when the average citizen has a few moments to dialogue with another, the only things that they feel safe discussing are the mundane common everyday experiences.

Yup these precious moments of uniqueness get spent regurgitating the boring moments of our own personal foibles.

The constant monetary necessity has perverted and permeated every area of our experience.

And there no longer exists such a thing as quiet contemplation for any sustained period.

Usually any outspoken rational questioning of our right to privacy, ultimately gets downplayed into a sitcom punchline.

Meanwhile children, friends, and neighbours turn in, ridicule, and isolate those who don't do all the right things, wear the right clothes, or watch the right TV shows and movies.

And we are made to feel that those behaviours are normal and that people have always been this way.

After all if you watch that big budget film about the good old days, those characters behaved very similar to us with the exception of their wardrobe and technologies.

That's to be expected in a culture where the truth is only acceptable when it benefits those already in power.

But let's get back to our elitest apathy.

The more that I consider the thought processes which shape the people that we become, the more I can see that modifying our behaviour is similar to modifying a word by putting the sounding stress on a different syllable.

In the same way that when we watch a film or television show the emphasis is placed on the action, sex appeal, etc.

Appealing to the lowest common denominator in order to maximize profits and minimize costs.

I suspect that the reason for this is similar to the reason why I personally never took a job working with computers.

I realized back in the early days of computing that if I spent a lot of time helping others fix their machines or spent prolonged periods doing mundane tasks which I didn't enjoy then I would be more reluctant to spend quality time creating 'puter stuff on my own.

In that same way we have chosen with our purchases which types of shows would be produced.

So since our days at work, in school, or at home with the kids are quite taxing mentally and emotionally.

Then when we have some *free time*, we don't want to think too much or feel anything negative.

And as a result we end up with these formulaic action shows and feel good one-liners but very little of the substance which might cause us to think too deeply about any serious subject.

Which is also another reason why we feel okay about getting drunk or high after work, because there won't be anything that we will really need to remember anyway.

I believe we need to focus on reversing these trends and get back to using the best parts of ourselves for the benefit of us all.

Which of course is easier to say than to do.

But thankfully there have been a number of pioneers in many of these areas. Of course many of the most successful ones and/or the ones which were ultimately a threat to the economic and/or political powers of the time have been marginalized/eliminated through various means.

So we need to rediscover, reinvigorate, and reeducate ourselves in these important fields and the tools which they can provide.

I mean just imagine a prolonged period of global peace by self-supported citizens with healthy food, practical non-negative impact health care, positive media and entertainment, etc.

If you can't, then you're not trying hard enough.

But hey that's just my opinion.

Do you have anything to contribute?

Or are you in training for the Apathy Olympics?

Ad Infinitum

To further elaborate on the many reasons for our current apathetic western culture, let's look at some of the larger groups and the various ways that those members get steered around the truth.

I was told by a friend long ago that I should write about what I know.

So we'll start with the most common reasons why people don't or won't read my writing.

First off there are the various forms of racists who don't want to hear about tolerance, equality, and inclusiveness.

That is a very effective money maker for the gun manufacturers and the rest of the armaments industry.

Second are the *end of the world* religious believers who's whole belief systems are built on the idea that we are living in the end times.

So they need there to be wars and religious persecutions or they would need to rethink their whole world view.

Third, of course we have the homophobes.

Ironically this includes those who are open about their beliefs and those who are *in the closet* about those beliefs as far as the rest of the world can see, but still carry around these beliefs whether actively or passively.

Fourth are those who believe that my views are politically incompatible with their own.

In North America this would would largely include those who consider themselves to be members of the major political parties.

In the USA this would be the Democrats and Republicans while in Canada they would include the Conservatives, Liberals, and NDP.

This is a perfect example of why people such as Kurt Cobain hated labels.

Fifth we have the wealthy who are quite simply afraid of losing what they themselves stole.

Sixth are the sexists who are fearful of women in any positions of power.

Seventh are the religious dogmatists who won't listen to anyone who isn't in strict adherence to their particular belief system.

Eighth are those who are in the infinite loop of drug and alcohol addiction. They don't want to hear about the reality of their situation because denial is a lot easier than change.

Ninth are those who can't read English, whether in whole or in part. This is the one group to which I owe an apology due to my own monoliguistic ability.

And also due to the fact that many of the references in my writing are time sensitive and culturally dependant, as most of it was intended for those in my own geographic area.

This list can certainly continue ad infinitum to include the lazy and selfish who rip off their friends and neighbours, etc.

But as always what it comes down to is INTENTIONS.

We all certainly have reasons daily to be angry, jealous, frustrated, isolated, etc.

And how we deal with it is the real purpose of our lives.

The Grand Idea was to put us complex, advanced, emotional, mortal beings into an open-ended system with the purpose of *learning to deal*.

Every single thing that you do matters, so human up already.

Help your neighbours and friends, stop being that needy, greedy, car speedy bastard and help us clear the next hurdle.

What the fuck else ya gonna do?

Immersed In The Trifecta

Immersed in the trifecta.

That perpetual motion machine of constant global warfare.

From a completely detached perspective devoid of emotion and morality it might appear elegant but certainly not beautiful, that would require the capacity for love.

I recently went back and started rewatching the James Bond films based on Ian Flemming's novels.

Of course Sean Connery is the best 007 and those films still stand up as great cinema.

But what really caught my attention right away was that the group known as *Spectre* is introduced in the first film in 1962.

Along with the idea that the best way to achieve certain goals was to play America and Russia off against each other.

That kind of sounds similar to what is going on right now, as more and more truth comes out through various means, Wikileaks, Anonymous, etc.

The corporate cartels and their minions are attempting to always bend, distort, and otherwise reshape the perceptions of the mass public.

Don't get me wrong, I am not claiming to have all the answers.

But I know full well that with just the information which I have had access to and a judicial system which is unbiased and not completely toothless where it counts...

Any group of rational non-brainwashed jurists would agree that there are a wide range of heinous crimes being perpetrated by those who, for whatever reason, feel that they are above the law.

It has gotten to the point now where recently a group from various American intelligence agencies has had enough of the corruption in the current government.

So they went ahead and got a hold of and leaked, via Wikileaks, a large number of incriminating emails related to the Presidential candidate who would carry on and expand upon the antics of the current government.

Loyal patriotic men and women put their careers in jeopardy because they had seen enough and realized that things weren't going to get any better unless someone made a timely act of rebellion.

Bravo for that and who knows exactly how much impact their defiance had, but that candidate did lose the election.

So the string of selfless actions done for the sake of a better humanity continues to grow.

It has been said that courage is contagious, which is precisely why the really courageous stuff isn't generally reported in the mainstream media.

And when it is reported or made reference to at all then there is always a derogatory spin attached.

It reminds me of the final months leading up to the end of World War Two in Germany.

The criminals currently in charge know full well that their reign is coming to an end, at least in their current positions of power.

So it is like when the Nazi hierarchy whipped their subordinates into a final fight-to-the-death mentality.

Meanwhile the compartmentalized structure allowed Hitler and many others to escape with their lives and much more.

While the weapons left behind were thrown at the advancing liberating forces.

I am quite sure that those who are now fighting against our pursuit of truth, freedom, and equality also have been duped into believing that they are fighting for a just cause.

Like I said before, we are immersed in the trifecta.

In George Orwell's 1984, there are three regions of the planet who are perpetually at war with each other.

The alliances and combatants would change but the one constant was the lack of peace.

That book was published in 1948 and although very prophetic, the geography has changed.

Instead of geographic regions like for example The Americas, Europe with Africa, and Asia with Australia or something similar and constantly changing...

What we have these days has evolved so that even though there are no longer two superpowers, we still have apparently two sides plus terrorism and the like.

But that is a carefully shaped illusion.

What we really have is America and its entourage versus all the rest.

And in situations where they can't drum up support for full scale wars like Iraq, Afghanistan, etc...

We see conflicts where *extremists* and *freedom fighters* clash for various reasons.

But later we learn that these groups were in fact supported by the larger powers who claimed at the time to be neutral.

Okay then, most people who have taken the time to try and understand what's going on will eventually arrive at a similar perspective.

However that illusion has been brought to us by the same people who have concealed Hitler and other high ranking Nazi's survival for many years after the war.

Because at another level of our human reality things like countries, religions, ethnicities, etc become nothing more that various colours of a rainbow.

On that stage all that matters is love or the lack of love which is commonly referred to as evil.

And those who gravitate towards wanting power for themselves at the expense of others obviously lack love.

The only force that can stand up to them is the power of love.

Which is why those who actually currently run the power game on this planet work in the shadows.

Because to maintain their consolidated power base they must consistently work the Machiavelli playbook and keep the two *geographic* powers perpetually at war.

While at the same time investing in both sides of each conflict and gaining massive profits regardless of who wins the battles.

It's a pretty fucked up situation!

And at this point I would love to be able to give you all a magic solution to fix these problems...

A Message From Our Sponsors

The propaganda wars are approaching a feverish intensity in the recent struggles for control over the sheep.

We really have been trained to be lazy in our day-to-day pursuit of information.

It has become both interesting and frustrating for me to watch other people's reactions to the distracting yarns being spun by the *various unscrupulous*.

Our love is a safety net, but it is our intentions which do the actual navigating of our reality.

So I have been disappointed by those who have initially seemed to share my values and purposes.

But they weren't content with truth, understanding, and moral fortitude.

Instead their pursuits tended towards sensational tabloid pablum which provided them with their daily justifications for inaction.

You see, they really didn't look far enough down the road for a decent solution to their situations.

They have now been turned into trivia junkies.

Anything shiny and fantastic to give them a rush and distract from their day-to-day servitude.

There's that short attention span again, the hidden ruler of so many minds.

I read something interesting today in the alternative news, which basically reminded me that we can't change *the systems* in control by using the tools provided by those *same systems*.

Also when someone thinks outside the box and begins to make a difference, that is the same as painting a target on their back.

If they can't be quietly bought out by *the corporations* then they are rendered ineffective using other means.

Which brings me to another huge issue that I haven't heard many others discuss, duality.

We are trained to believe that for most situations there are only two choices.

Light versus dark, good versus evil, positive and negative, etc.

The grey area or *middle ground* scares the hell out of the powers-that-be.

You see, if there are only two sides to a situation, then to maintain control all you need to do is control both.

So when people try to *rebel* in the fashions sold to them (drinking, smoking, drugs, etc), what most don't realize is that the people running the *dark side* are in fact part of the same system which they are attempting to escape/change/rebel against.

Which is what is meant when those who get disenchanted say that *the system is rigged*.

The *War On Drugs* was the same as any other war, just an announcement of who would be in control of a certain situation.

And I'm not talking about the victors either, because most of the wars aren't declared for a final outcome to be decided.

There are always numerous reasons for any major *war*, and it is never for the publicly declared reasons.

So basically Earth is now being run like a big farm and we peasants are the livestock.

I mean just consider that we have, according to mainstream knowledge, been capable of landing on the Moon since the late 1960s.

When my mind roams and ponders the numerous possibilities that an additional 40 years could have brought...

Well now as they said on *The X-files*, the truth is out there.

And it is becoming clearer every day that there may have been extraterrestrial contact at some point but the majority of sightings are of man-made craft.

It has simply been convenient to allow the public to chase aliens, demons, satanists, etc.

We have all become actors auditioning for the parts that will pay our bills.

Some of us remain in local productions, while others gain more worldly notoriety.

But we must continue to act the parts which we have been allotted.

Like the pets and farm animals that we are, we must go through the motions to receive our daily feedings.

Which I suppose is one of the main reasons why when someone gets fed up and goes on a truth telling tirade, no one really seems to have a clue how to respond.

That wasn't in the script, so let's break for lunch and wait for *security* to sort it out.

There that's better, food clothing shelter pharmaceuticals and *security*.

We really don't deserve any better anyway, seeing as we are all born sinners.

Pretty fucking sad if you think about it, but we haven't got time to think about it and there are pills to keep us happy.

Okay, time for a commercial break with a *message* from our sponsors.

Global Love Saturation

Don't think, don't dream, and certainly don't try to imagine anything better.
There's no room for that in our Fascist Reich, and whatever the equivalents
are for the Communists and Capitalists.

Everything has been organized so that we must perpetually earn our basic
human rights, they are no longer considered our birth rights.

You and I both know, when we take the time to really think about it, that
each of our lives is a unique and amazing expression of love's potential.

But with the unchecked expansion of corporate financial domination, most
of us have been conditioned on multiple levels to believe that we aren't
deserving of an equal share in our collective earthly experience.

Meanwhile an occasional *beautiful mind* will see through many of those
lies.

And they will try to point out this faulty logic to their friends and family but
without much effect.

You see, real power is gained with patience and persistence.

So I really do have to give our overlords credit, they have learned from
some of their ancestors' mistakes.

There are literally no areas of our day to day experience that aren't
overwhelmingly influenced by the corporate agendas.

And while it might be tempting to get all worked up about the crazy, selfish,
and downright evil antics of highly publicized individuals such as
celebrities, cops, politicians, or the weekly mass murderers.

The truly dangerous actions are taken behind closed doors by the puppets
wearing suits.

They are really just as expendable to the real powers as we are.

Which raises the issue of privacy.

Ultimately the invasions of our privacy and supposedly confidential
information are the tools which are used to manipulate these corporate
pawns into positions of power.

Oh sure the corporate funded films, television series, and *news* articles will
paint a picture of our so called leaders as regular folk who worked hard to
achieve their lofty positions.

Or maybe it was similar to winning the lottery, they were just good honest citizens in the right place at the right time.

If either of those scenarios was even remotely true, the global situation would have started to head in the right direction long ago.

But like any example of unchecked power, inevitably disaster ensues for their victims.

As so often happens, I have painted yet another canvas which portrays a dire situation and many will try at this point to flip the painting over with hopes that the answer is inscribed on the back...

But alas the answer to this problem has yet to be written.

I mean just look at the recent legislation passed in America which protects corporations like Monsanto from having to easily visibly label the foods which contain GMO ingredients.

And while myself and many of the people reading or listening to this have made an effort to sift through the layers of shit showered upon us daily, what becomes of it?

Once again we must reflect upon the staggering amounts of money thrown towards Corporate Propaganda and Black Ops Wet Work.

Another example is the many holistic healers and doctors who have been working for cures to diseases such as Cancer, etc.

Many in the past year have either *disappeared* or committed *suicide* soon after announcing breakthrough cures.

Do the math, an approximately $5000 contract hit on some civilian versus Big Pharma's annual income from Cancer alone.

It doesn't take a rocket scientist to figure out the probable outcome.

And the examples go on and on.

It is the *Thunderdome* mentality on a global scale, just keep the peasants broke, hungry, and turn a select few into attack dogs who will gladly answer the call for a chance to advance out of the mud.

So once again we get back to the issue of the futility of we the few struggling to improve not only our lot, but various possible improvements across the board.

Because as we all know, when we give everyone a minimally humane standard of living then the money needed to spend on Armies, Drugs, and Prisons goes way down.

There have been many examples in other countries recently and from our past which bear these ideas out as fact.

But as always in this modern banking monopolistic fascism that we live in, unless there is a profit to be made by those at the top of the power pyramid, then things don't change.

So as I have pointed out numerous times, in order to make a corporation change we must make it financially beneficial for them to do so.

This can be done in many ways so be creative, because the main weapons that we have are love and creativity.

And as always, these actions will benefit from long-term strategy and global cooperation.

Because small pockets of resistance scattered randomly will fall like raindrops.

Whereas a collection of this gravity induced moisture can be poured out as a torrent with a larger impact and a much longer duration.

Again these are only broad outlines, the trick is to remain ahead of their ability to effectively defend.

And of course a disclaimer is needed round about now because, taken out of context, this could sound rather *terrorist* like.

However, what I am proposing is 100% physically passive.

Economic sanctions against rogue corporations, and things like the passive *standing protests* which I have recently heard about happening around the globe.

That reminds me of a topic which is sure to be controversial.

I don't really know what the propaganda is like in other areas of the world, but here in CanAmerica (Canada & USA) the suggestions which we are bombarded with lately are that only the rich and morally compromised are supposed to have children.

Meanwhile the rest of us dirty peasants are rendered sterile, unworthy, and selfish.

We should be happy to have the opportunity to adopt the orphaned children from the countries which the corporations have recently raped of their resources.

And again I am not lacking compassion for those displaced by these demonic wars of aggression.

I say we can and should both heal the sick and prevent the disease that is war.

Or how about the push to legalize euthanasia of the elderly and infirmed? The students of history should see a scary parallel to the Eugenics movements in the past of which the Nazis were obviously huge supporters.

Also, getting back to children, pregnancy, and families.

It is really disturbing how many children are born to single moms.

Or the high percentages of dads who aren't the biological fathers, raising children they believe are actually theirs.

Consider for a moment the profound sickness of a society which not only condones but actually promotes drunken one night stands as a right of passage.

And look even deeper into the types of *people* who own the nightclubs, breweries, and drug cartels which help to orchestrate this massive mind fuck!

As always it is up to us, because the good people in positions of power are completely outnumbered.

It is time we had their backs, as our acts of love for all will be recognized and reinforced.

It seems like most people don't really know how to participate.

So be a leader towards the global love saturation...

Push Up

Here we go again, missing the point entirely.

The great majority of those vocal opponents now bitching about Trump seem oblivious to the reasons why so many people were disenchanted with the previous regime.

Let's pause and take some time to really examine why they won't even consider that both of their parties are seriously flawed and further that the current overarching political structure is damaged beyond repair (at least from the perspective of the 99%).

I recently watched a video clip of a Trump supporter arguing with someone who was strongly opposed to most of what he stands for.

It was pretty silly theatre really, but what I found to be the most illuminating were the comments from the overwhelmingly pro Trump supporters posted underneath this YouTube video.

I imagine that it would have been similar to the jokes and rhetoric of skinheads.

It started off quite tame, but once the participants recognized that they were in a mostly pro Trump forum, well then they opened up with how they really felt.

You know, the same old presumptions of superiority and violently aggressive threats and put downs.

The American two party system is now at the point where both of their extremist leaderships are so violently opposed to the other side that there can't be any common ground for the foreseeable future.

Which I firmly believe is what those who own that country really want.

They fully support both sides to an extreme so that either of the top two sides on its own is more powerful than the third, fourth, fifth, etc parties combined.

Its like Formula One racing where the fastest two cars are owned by the same people.

The rest are just there for show.

The craziest thing from my perspective is that as more and more people in *foreign* countries wake up to the American Dream/Nightmare, those living in the United/ Forever Divided States seem to dig in and get more entrenched in their apparent ignorance.

But I suppose this happens in all empires as they head towards their downfall.

Now this is where the pro USA camp starts to say that those of us naysayers are simply jealous and hoping to gobble up pieces after the collapse.

I would respond by saying that what we are really hoping for is that the American military jackboots get removed from our throats so that we can start to breath regular again.

That would be a good start.

Also I would point out that myself and my friends aren't the ones that consistently resort to violence as the preferred solution for most of our disagreements.

But to truly *change* the situation, we must reconstruct the main pillars of a system which is so completely toxic that it is a lot like the annual cleaning of the household fridge and freezer.

In these cases we need to crack open some containers that we would prefer to leave closed.

But in good conscience, we need to be thorough.

It occurs to me that what has been repeatedly happening down through the decades is that as the new leaders come into office, they are informed that the price of winning is that they can't open certain containers.

You know the same old same old, like when we allow the police to prosecute cases of their own police brutality.

And it usually ends up being some decent officer who wants to do the right thing who ends up being thrown to the wolves as an appeasement so that those at the heart of the corruption can point and say that they care.

"You will know them by their fruits."

So how do we get to a system where those in positions of *leadership* are decent, loving, caring, etc?

A short-term solution seems quite difficult.

However, in the long-term, we would be well advised to come clean regarding all aspects of our society so that the next generation can formulate a realistic future.

Seeing as what has been happening for many years is that the children are being raised on fairy tales and cartoons while school isn't much more realistic.

Then finally when they leave the cocoon and enter the real world, they are completely unprepared and either fall back to their families for support or end up doing whatever they have to do in order to survive.

So nothing really changes and they just continue the two-faced legacy, perpetuating the great collective lie.

Humans living without humanity, but it doesn't have to be this way.

The nice part about hitting the bottom is that now we have something to push up from...

Take The Hint

So you say that you want me to be ambitious.

And I ask if you are prepared to lead.

But not just me, are you ready to lead by example?

Can you look past your own ambition, your own self, and see that we are all one.

Yes even the assholes, like one big dysfunctional family.

Has anyone that you respected ever challenged you to be more than just a stereotype?

Generally what I see collectively at this moment is a bunch of self interested children sneaking around and scamming each other.

And then in their inevitable future decline, they will feign ignorance as to the roots of their maladies and cancers.

Or to the fact that many of the drug overdoses which are so common these days are in fact targeted hits by one racist group or another.

Come on you dumbed down lazy consumers, do something about that cesspool of an environment which you wade through on the daily.

At some point we all need to unplug our usual distractions and do the things which we all agreed to do before we came into our lives.

Yes I know it all seems pointless, futile, and even naively silly at times.

But do you really want to continue living a sedated conformist life, while helping to enslave your fellow inmates?

Oops sorry about that, I distracted you from nothing at all really.

But as you begin to focus on what I am doing and saying, it is starting to make sense and that scares the living shit out of you.

Because if even just a little bit of it is true then that presents the idea that you might need to alter your life.

And we all know that life is hard enough, so we sure don't look forward to the extra burden that a revolutionary mindset would bring.

But come on now, are you really comfortable with POTUS playing Russian roulette with the nuclear weapons?

I know it appears rather hopeless at times and the powers-that-be seem to have a contingency plan for anything us peasants can possibly dream up.

But that is mostly smoke, mirrors, and impossible bluffs.

What are they gonna do...

    1. Claim that the entire population of the planet are terrorists?

    2. Declare global martial law based on their own false flag alien invasion?

    3. Systematically bankrupt *Rogue Nations* (those countries which refuse to bow down to the US dollar or Rothschild central banks) and then blame the leaders

of those countries for the poverty of their people?

4. Generate selective genocides using weather modification and sociopaths?

5. Eliminate potential whistle blowers, civil rights activists, brave documentarians and journalists, etc using backdoors and wiretaps on all our sources of communication?

You get the point.

Like Dan Aykroyd said in the film Sneakers, "It's not a question of whether you are paranoid, but whether you are paranoid enough."

But nevermind all that, let's go shopping so we can pretend to be cool and smart trendsetters, then everyone will look up to and envy us.

I mean the rest of the world doesn't deserve our help and respect or so we've been taught.

All that matters is how we feel and how others feel about us, right?

Sometimes I feel like I am in that scene in the Matrix where Morpheus is explaining to Neo the reality of the situation.

"Most of the population aren't ready to be woken up."

I remember when I was a kid and I really wanted answers to the whos, whats, whys, wheres, and whens.

But the only answers available were from sanitized victor's history books and overly paranoid drug addicts who had inhaled far too much misinformation to present a helpful picture.

Like military basic training, our socioeconomic system isolates us right from the start of our lives and then trains us to believe that we never have enough of all those things which we are told that we need.

In our culture this has been going on so long that most of us truly believe that these traits which have been grafted onto us are actually just our basic human nature.

And while some people concern themselves with the idea that people are accepting and incorporating more and more machines into their lives everyday and are thereby becoming more *physically* machine-like.

In fact that situation has already been going on and is further advanced *emotionally* and *psychologically*.

So it is simply a case now of our hybrid exterior catching up to its interior.

And most simply ingest this information like another Hollywood film, something to watch but not participate in.

While there are a very small percentage who view it like a documentary and try to incorporate some of the new material into their daily lives.

Take the hint!

Picked Off

I gotta say that at this point I am getting really fucking tired of all you selfish bitches trying to take everything for yourselves and fucking everyone else over in the process.

So no more virtual reality video games for you.

Now for a global timeout on these legions of overgrown toddlers.

You have forfeited your rights beyond personal daily needs, food clothing and shelter.

I think that we need to put you all into complete detoxes and rehabs until qualified councillors determine that your emotional, psychological, and physical levels have become *humane* again.

And before all you stoners and drunks get all bent out of shape, what we are talking about here goes way beyond drug addiction.

*The definition of Addiction - "A brain disorder characterized by compulsive engagement in rewarding stimuli despite adverse consequences."

So I think it is pretty obvious that with a little contemplation and an open mind concerning the maniacs who have been slowly but surely turning the planet into a global sanitarium where things have been turned upside down...

Power, sex, adrenaline, drugs, sugar, fat, caffeine, etc.

Now usually when I start to point out a long list like this, people will commonly try to dismiss it by saying "well everything is addictive!"

And I can see how that might appear to be simplistically true on a cursory glance into our western culture.

But that is in large part due to the capitalist/consumer profit motive.

Like the way that big box stores have pushed out smaller stores and family businesses.

In the same way, only the super profitable and super addictive products and services are left.

For the most part it isn't individuals deciding to screw over their fellow humans in conscious sweeping villainous acts.

But rather it is an inevitable consequence of the market economics which we have witnessed grossly engulfing our civilizations.

So many metaphors pop into my mind, which is itself rather disturbing because this means that these situations haven't been rare in our history and also that we haven't seemed to put a priority on preventing such recurrences.

Now one of the major reasons why I am so actively trying to wake up such an enormous amount of our civilization at once is because I have noticed recently that when only a small amount of good people pop up here and there then they are getting picked off with *cancers, suicides, car accidents, etc.*

But a larger number would be harder to quietly eliminate.

Speaking of cancer, I have recently found it to be rather ironic that the push to legalize marijuana has been accompanied by claims that the drug actually cures cancers and various other ailments.

Now I don't know whether these wondrous claims are in fact valid.

But I do find it ironic that on a certain level we have been conditioned to believe that in order to live a *healthy* life we must be drugged in one way or another.

It reminds me of the old idea that we have to *fight for peace.*

There's that lack of mainstream critical thinking again.

Okay stop me if you've heard this one before, but maybe we should focus on finding what is causing these cancers in the first place.

Peter Joseph pointed out many interesting things in his new book, *The New Human Rights Movement.*

But the point that I was just reminded of was when he was talking about the philanthropy of the rich.

The fact that philanthropy is even necessary means that the economic systems which we have in place aren't working properly.

So instead of relying on a small *elite* group to fix the problems which they are completely emotionally and physically detached from, maybe we should empower those in the *trenches* who are longing for the chance to truly help their friends and family.

But that has the outside possibility of equalizing the economic situations of all involved which is why it is resisted by those at the top of the pyramid.

And like the way that they have used the legal, medical, and psychiatric systems to *protect the lower classes from hurting themselves*, we need to collectively restrain these power junkies from hurting themselves and others while they are *tripping.*

Unless I am completely missing the reasons why they think that they are so much better than us.

Here's a good idea for a reality TV show, take the wealthiest 100 people on the planet under the age of 50 and force them to be homeless for a year.

Let's see that refined pedigree in action.

Any predictions on the outcome?

Actually, I am only joking.

Odds are that they would literally die of culture shock or would kill themselves from bouts of depression.

God damn it, there are so many things in our culture which attempt to train us to value ourselves and our possessions over others.

Which can be seen played out on the global stage as the constant posturing of the various state powers against each other.

And as the media outlets, which are in effect state owned much like an Orwellian nightmare, bombard us unceasingly with noisy mind-numbing technicolor shit.

Then when crucial events take place which the global population need to be properly informed about, we are instead deluged with various forms of disinformation.

Like in the recent Manchester bombing, where the important history of the *terrorists* is whitewashed.

And we are told to believe that he/they were just more crazy hateful Muslims.

No mention of the environment of death and oppression which they grew up in.

Obviously bombing innocent civilians at a concert is horrible.

But exploiting the anger and grief from that tragedy or any other similar situation is also morally questionable.

And with the last century full of so many false flag operations that the generally accepted history is in most cases an agreed upon fantasy compared to what actually happened...

It makes a person stop and really question the facts of any major impacting event.

Another interesting topic which could potentially become a future scenario, zombies.

Seriously, what is the fascination that we have with a *zombie apocalypse*?

I realize that it sounds kinda silly, but what if we are being conditioned to believe in the possibility of it happening?

Kind of like asteroids, alien invasions, and rogue nations.

For example, let's say that there happens to be a popular global uprising and the rich elite upper-classes are on the run from the karma of their sins.

A final solution to save their own asses could be to hide in their airtight bunkers and earth homes while a Resident Evil-like zombie pathogen is released to cull us *unruly* masses?

Remember that most films are based on at least a small kernel of truth!

Pleasant dreams...

Innocent

Sunshine, warmth, and time to myself.

Okay then, let's give up on the revolution, settle down and raise some fluoridated children.

What I need is to watch some prime time television so that the commercials can coerce me into buying a future full of planned obsolescence.

After all there isn't any chance for us slaves to free ourselves from the multileveled nightmare that most aren't even aware of.

I so enjoy my daily commute to a job which is full of tasks which are morally questionable.

And I enjoy being forced to work with people who are constantly looking for ways to screw each other over.

I am enjoying the life that I am allowed to live, really!?

Sometimes it feels like the only thing this life has trained me to do is lie about how I feel.

I mean we wouldn't get much *work* done if we honestly answered when someone else asked us a question...

How are you doing?

Would it be be alright if...?

What are you gonna do tonight?

Nope that can't happen, we must bury that honesty deep down.

Like all the truths of the past which have become the foundation of this holographic collective self-delusion.

It seems that it might be nice if we sent the ignorant innocents on a short vacation (aka The Rapture) while the Darkness and the Light battle it out once and for all.

But that's one of the major tragedies in this theatre.

The power and momentum of the dark propaganda has actually enlisted the majority of the population without their knowledge.

Consider the soldiers who have gone to another country for what they believe are good reasons.

Only to finish their tours and realize that they were fighting on the wrong side.

And there are countless examples from virtually every occupation.

I mean wow, just consider the scope of the global mind fuck which happens every single day for this generation!

But don't worry, have a hot shower, put on some clean clothes, grab that high-interest credit card and go find some new distraction to get you through the night.

But never ever give in to the emotions which scream at you every single fucking second.

Certainly no one else will want to hear it or even care.

You are all alone in this crowd of comfortable sheep.

Occasionally one of them catches your eye, but it is only on the surface.

Like a polygon character in the FPS of your choice.

Just another hollow distraction.

I know you are filled with a multitude of excuses for your behaviour.

That is something which you have to live with.

Consider the irony of purchasing a self-help book...

It seems that mostly you are only helping yourself to the cash register.

Your head is filled with short-term strategies to achieve your next quick fix.

If I didn't understand the majority of the reasons for your behaviour, then I might hold you more responsible.

But really your actions and emotions are so predictable that your strings are easy to manipulate.

Oh I know, you have been sold the *free will* perspective.

But really, in your current situation, you are like a character in GTA going on about how "The world is your oyster".

Or a *synthetic* in Blade Runner with a built in expiration date and someone else's memories.

So many artists have pulled apart our individual tragedies while high on some particular chemical composition.

We earn our bread and water by selling each other out and poisoning people we've never met.

But so long as everyone else is doing it we are all innocent, right?!

Multiple Choice

Okay let's not constantly look back at our individual histories with nostalgia and revisionist doctored wishful thinking.

Some like to think of our current global chaos as a school, but while essentially true, that is also a rather childish cop out.

Because the ultimate lesson and learning experience would be to pull our collective asses out of the fire and organize, create, and dream ourselves into an environment of multi-spectrum illumination?

But alas the understandings necessary for the vast multitude of personalities populating this marvellous marble we live on are being systematically turned into punchlines and topics of ridicule.

Sometimes it really seems like there are two different realities.

One which is visible to the passive majority and another which is only seen by an isolated minority.

And no I really don't believe that either of the two is at its core more important, more powerful, more deserving, or more in any other way.

Humanity can be seen as a deck of cards where each person has a different face value and suit.

Or an even closer analogy would be to imagine a symbolic human big bang where each *individual* is initially composed of a slightly different mass, direction, and velocity.

Essentially we all were initially one and actually still are if only farther apart.

Presently for various reasons the majority are simply unable to either see, understand, or feel empowered enough to change their situation.

Simply the luck of the draw, it could be said, has blinded them to these truths.

And of course, if any of us take the time to stop and look around ourselves with good intentions, then we will surely come to similar conclusions based on our own observations.

So don't wade out of this current of apathy, because the truth can be a heavy burden.

It has been sold to the masses as a delusional insanity, etc.

But the real insanity is in beliefs such as:

-we can vote for change.

-the economic system will self-correct for the benefit of the 99%.

-the majority of our world population are really violent and blood-thirsty.

-some benevolent god will look favourably on a chosen group and either intercede on their behalf by destroying their enemies or take that *best* group to somewhere better.

Recently we have seen the old Nazi brainwashing rising to the surface again.

You know that old thought process of blaming another race, religion, country, etc for the problems of a *chosen* group.

So with that belief, all that is needed is a genocidal wave to cleanse the planet of these *subhumans* and make the situation better.

Yup I know, even my creative thinking couldn't make this shit up.

It is a tried and tested formula which has been used repeatedly on those with a limited understanding of historical and present reality.

So much for education being the magic bullet to save us.

If truth was the only information out there then more knowledge would of course help.

But we currently have a situation where there are multiple distorted versions of the same events as well as the truth.

And people have the option to choose which version of the news that they want to watch, read, hear, and accept.

The majority of our most talented artists have sold out at various times to the corporations which have tons of money invested in keeping the most revolutionary truths hidden from us peasants.

Recently I have been encouraged by the counter-racism protests and I hope they will continue to remain peaceful.

I also hope that we can expand that enthusiasm to include many more issues.

But I suppose part of the reason why that issue is so popular and others aren't is because we have had experience combating Nazis in the past.

Whereas many of the other current issues are so new that most people don't recognize their true significance in our current predicament and the importance of combating them earlier rather than later.

So further along, when issues rise to the surface for many, we will still be mostly unsure how to mobilize our counter effects.

Which is sadly ironic when we look at the many genocides which our tax dollars are funding regularly and sold to us with various government propagandas.

While these actions themselves are a major issue that we need to stop participating in.

It almost seems like yesterday was our last chance, and waking up this morning we are left with the options for various forms of damage control.

Multiple choice anyone?!

The Slayer

Ready to be stunned, dazzled, and amazed?
Go fuck yourself!
That shit's in the gutter down the street.
All I've got for you are the reality chewables refined from the truths and
freedoms which your *soul* craves.
So you better get ready for your *body's* cravings to adopt the fight or flight
responses that have regularly maintained an inability to get above the
invisible ceiling of nowhere special.
And get set to have your *mind* distract you with all those preprogrammed
worries and tangents.
After all, we have made up legendary lists of how things work in each of
our *individual* universes and the love lob which I have catapulted your way
sure isn't recognized as being safe by your *player's* security forces.
I know it all sounds hopeless but don't worry.
Because it is already inside you and I am simply waking it up.
Just get up and stretch your body, mind, and soul.
Take a deep breath and smile, cuz I'm hittin' you with the wake up call that
we both agreed upon.
So quit bitching about the so-called bad timing.
And I ain't hearing any of the old apathetic *I'm doing okay* mantras.
Not to get all mystical on your ass, but if you are hearing and feeling me at
all then you have already made your choice.
That choice was yes, by the way.
A mutual agreement that we all made to do the things which are necessary
to get us where we need to go.
Just to clarify our situation, what is now coming to the surface in each of us
are not individual plans but rather awakenings and empowerings of the
unique eternal gifts that we each possess.
I suppose at this point it might be beneficial to learn how to use these gifts
in order to be prepared when necessary.
It also would be smart to really recognize your true tendencies and long-
term goals in order to avoid future self-defeating behaviours.

Because as we strengthen our gifts and abilities, we not only become capable of doing more general good but we also magnify our missteps.

One of those misused sayings of the past was "If it feels good do it."

But if we take that idea as a widely inclusive philosophy, then much good can be achieved.

So put away this life's short-term grievances and navigate your way out of those personal tragedies like someone sight-restricted following sounds, smells, touch, etc.

In this way, if we truly feel our way with unmuddled intentions it becomes inevitable that we will prevail on any humane adventure.

Ya I know, this is starting to sound rather cultish or religious.

But here are some of the major differences.

I am not trying to get anything from you, not trying to change who you are, and not trying to convince you of anything which either you don't already know or which isn't readily provable to yourself.

But if none of this sounds appealing, then the one thing that I do ask is that you stay out of our way.

We aren't looking for either the religious war or the good vs evil Armageddon which has been sold and refined for the masses over the millennia.

We have simply exhausted all the normal scenarios which have been presented as a means of arbitrating our grievances.

And we have travelled so far beyond those choices that they now seem old stories passed down through the generations.

Now shipwrecked in *the now* we have lost all our old baggage and approach this scene with fresh eyes and ears.

What if we could go to the Moon for the weekend, or Mars for a holiday?

What if all the lost souls could come up for a breath of fresh reality and we could all be one, not just in our dreams?

What if we could sidestep the negative thugs, banksters, corporate politicians, and various other members of the Army of the Dead?

What if there was enough love channelled through us all that the inevitable good simply fell into place?

Or if ideas which were negative towards the global good were just fleeting nonsense, in the same way most conspiracy (facts) theories are treated in mainstream thought currently?

Yup certainly sounds too good to be true, right?

But keep in mind that the enslavement of mass populations takes far more work.

I mean think about it, when was the last time that you had a conversation with another member of the 99% where there wasn't a majority of commonality between you two?

Certainly at present we are structured towards following leaders, so how do we get to a not so distant step in our human evolution where our *leaders* are entirely answerable to those they *serve*?

Sure beats the hell out of celebrity gossip and pro sports.

It has been said that we have to decide what we are prepared to give up to create a more just society.

But if we are all just individually perpetually chasing after our next adventure...

That sure doesn't leave much time to collectively make those big choices, let alone physically set them in motion.

Don't get me wrong, life is for living certainly.

But the lives that we *the privileged* currently enjoy come with a huge responsibility to those suffering in poverty, genocides, fascism, racism, sexism, etc.

If our current world drama was made into a Hollywood horror movie, we would be the vampires.

I don't know about you, but I always saw myself siding with *The Slayer*.

As always, these choices are ours to make.

Three Guesses

So today I'm in the mood for a little pleasant speculation and wishful thinking.
How about it, are you interested in trying to visualize something better?
We tend to get caught up in the multitude of negative comments, and to a certain extent we have become truth addicts.
Unfortunately the truth has been rather grim of late.
But let's take some time today and make a leap of faith that we can together overcome these obstacles and come out the far side of these struggles.
That oh so dangerous thing called hope.
If we can believe that we will inevitably prevail against any and all adversity then hope can once again be a gift.
So let's get on with building and creating an improved now and an enlightened future.
I'm not talking about a little home renovation and having enough money to be your own boss.
Nope, what we need is a lofty elevation above the smog of our current neighbourhood's ecosystem.
Outlandish inspiration is where it's at.
And in my experience, that kind of thinking starts with love.
For partners, children, family, community, and ever expanding to encompass at a minimum the entire planet.
Which, if you think about it, is why those who are currently creating the world around us aren't meeting the needs of the less privileged.
Because in the same way that those sleazy lawyers and corrupt politicians are the ones who are making our Orwellian laws...
The buildings, parks, and various neighbourhoods are being designed by those who are quite detached from the needs of the many.
Anyway, a *safe nurturing environment* is the common go-to description that the politically correct regurgitate when forced to verbalize some thought on this subject.
And of course the needs of each person will be unique.
So at the very least the environment must include non-toxic air, water, food, lighting, power, sound, etc.
Then once we get past the basics, we are left with the freedom to enjoy our unique social dynamics which will of course continue to evolve infinitely.
As for architecture, finance, education, transportation, fashion, entertainment, etc.

Well, I believe most would agree that there has been far too much economic segregation as to what each person can access.

This is where most of the material first world tends to tune out as they assume that I am suggesting taking from them to give to those less fortunate.

But lately the multitude of hurricanes and the hellish infernos of forest fires have reminded us how fleeting this wealth really is.

So if you want to be that selfish bastard who locks out the rest of the world while you hide inside of a fully self-sufficient bunker as the unnecessary wars, genocides, famines, and diseases exterminate the majority of humankind...

I will now pause for dramatic effect to give you time to consider an alternate strategy.

Come on, let's find some common ground.

Which brings us back to visualizing something better.

Stop falling for all those divide and rule manipulations which keep the races, genders, religions, countries, etc from working together.

We are consistently shown false *stories* about how one *group* or another is out to get us.

But in reality all we need do is follow the money to see who is really the cause of most of this chaos.

The current system of global economics can't sustain peace, plain and simple.

Humanity's moral evolution demands some radical changes.

Consider how much sickness and death is caused by anger and depression.

Meanwhile those who have the power to alter the system for the better are the same ones who benefit from the situation remaining the same.

It is the ultimate catch 22 situation, which I dare say is the way that the 1% like it.

Sure there are going to be some who will only tune in for 30 seconds and say that we are just being naive and paranoid.

It occurs to me that we can really use an honest educational curriculum which covers most if not all of the basics and the major lies and mind fucks.

Of course there will be many fringe issues that will not be included.

But definitely the underlying reasons for most wars and the real mechanics of our economic and political systems.

Making docs like *Citizenfour* essential viewing.

Also, we've had enough of the patriotic bullshit to defend useless imaginary borders.

I mean, really, turn off CNN and take most of the Hollywood propaganda with a healthy dose of skepticism.

I'm not siding with the *terrorists* but rather I *am* siding with *all* humanity.
In much the same way that most of us recognized that equal mediation was
necessary in the previous struggle between Ireland and England.
So we should think globally and act locally with respect to the *economic gang*
violence perpetrated all the way from the level of the street up to the violence
between *nations* and *terrorists*.
Don't get me wrong it's not all *organized*, but the random acts of violence are tiny in
comparison and are in fact usually byproducts of the larger problems.
Most of those involved at the lower levels recognize this and that is why
indoctrination and compartmentalization are such handy and popular organizational
tools for the so-called *underground*.
However even after discussing all these things globally and coming to a majority
agreement with the 99%, the problem still remains that at present the systems in
place are rigged in favour of the 1%.
Okay so here's a hypothetical, albeit all too plausible scenario:
What if a nuclear device were to detonate in the ocean off either the west or east
coasts of the United States and the blame was placed on China?
Regardless of whether it was true, the ensuing Tsunami would kill more than we can
imagine and retaliation would happen long before a thorough investigation could be
completed.
And while the U.S. Military Industrial Intelligence Complex roars into overdrive,
why not go after those *rogue* nations who have recently dropped the U.S. Dollar?
There you go, a two-for-one sale on world domination.
One thing that I learned from watching MacGyver and 007 is that anything is
possible if you have the right tools.
So who has access to these sorts of weapons and compartmentalized black op wet
work teams capable of instigating such a heinous act and not only get away with it,
but also place the blame on the desired parties?
You get three guesses and the first two don't count.

Unremember

So we keep ourselves distracted and tired with the hopes that others will fix the world for us.

As if somehow they can see our unique issues and emotions.

And once perceived, our desires are then catapulted to the top of their to-do lists.

Of course, it is quite apparent that these behaviours which we continue to repeat are rooted in the childhood indoctrinations which have repeatedly told us that those in power should be heeded and respected.

Like the old 1984 propaganda says, *ignorance is bliss*.

What is the difference between actors in a fascist propaganda film, verses your personal apathy?

They both promote the same results, which is why *knowledge is power*.

Because when we are properly informed on most of the factors in a situation, then we can *play out the tape* and see the long-term effects of our actions.

Most people have had occasion to get upset on a regular basis, and when they look at the overwhelming negative results of rebellion then they usually give up.

But when they have an informed perspective, then multiple options present themselves and maybe, just maybe a positive outcome becomes achievable.

Hope is what we are searching for at this point.

We have dug such a deep hole that rainbows and unicorns are a long way off.

The path is long and twisted, so for the time being we will advance in small increments.

Of course at the same time it is important that we don't lose ground in other areas.

We are the multi-spectrum *light* which can be focused by a common purpose into a *sabre* of peace and truth.

Remember to *unremember* our negative programming which has trained us to look for a charismatic leader to follow.

Be the best version of yourselves and realize that we are at a crucial time and we are truly defined by how we influence those around us.

It is not a matter of being that plastic politician who appears to be perfectly presentable.

But rather, being an engaged individual who is strong enough to be alone but always an integral part of the whole that is us.

We are organizing, evolving, and learning from our mistakes and triumphs. Is it enough?

Can we find our lost hope?

Are we prepared to do the work required?

Once again it bears repeating that we are in a global top-down hierarchy. *Everybody knows*, you sure got that right Leonard Cohen.

The examples which are readily apparent to myself and my friends, are situations like what has been and is still happening to Julian Assange.

Help others to do the right thing and become hunted by one of the largest clandestine groups of ruthless thugs on the planet.

Then we have Edward Snowden, who saw first-hand from the inside what happens in today's global reality when *absolute power corrupts absolutely*.

He was prepared to sacrifice his career, freedom, and relationships to try and make any difference that was within his power.

Recently, citizens in Spain decided by a majority vote to make a change in how things are done.

So the Spanish Federal Government stepped in and jailed those they considered to be responsible and denied their citizens the results of their own democratic vote.

But don't worry about that, the winter holidays are coming and we need to save up for the latest iPhone, etc.

When was the last time that you seriously even considered protesting something?

Do you not have any issues with the current situation?

I don't mind admitting that the overwhelming popular apathy by those whom I encounter everyday is by far the most perplexing, frustrating, and discouraging part of my day.

Just thinking about it now is almost enough to make me put down the pen and paper.

But by now those reading or listening to this are familiar with my eternal optimism.

If only I could make that trait of mine contagious.

Then, like a Bond villain, I could spread it globally and watch the whole world heal itself at once.

But where's the fun in that?

Why won't you set some lofty goals to achieve?

What is it that you are really afraid of deep down?

Oops, I guess you probably just changed the channel.

There are plenty of *people* willing to tell you what you want to hear.

I mean really, you deserve to be happy.

No really, you sold your soul long ago.

So now that you struggle every day with your morally questionable job requirements, you certainly deserve to be happy in your *free time*.

Yup, you deserve it all right!

Don't for a second turn off your phone, lock your door, and cover the cameras on your laptop and cable box.

Because maybe, just maybe you will then have a humane thought about something other than yourself and the products that you are being conditioned to want.

And the funny thing is that the only ones still reading this or hearing it are the ones who already know this shit!

My intention is not to acquire enough *wealth* to buy the life which is being sold.

But rather to use what is already *inside* to discover the life which is being hidden.

Never Ever

So, maybe take some time to figure out what your vision of a better reality would be.

Then get back to doing your normal routine.

Let some time pass and give a first revision to the original ideas.

Then when you get stumped again, take a good long break.

Followed once again by another recursive revision, and on and on...

You get the point.

Okay now stop reading this and only return when you are mildly content with those revisions.

Right then, now think about those things which survived all the revisions, not necessarily the new stuff.

The core stuff is what we will focus on for this initial burst of personal creation.

These will be the things which you are now personally responsible for building in our collective reality.

There must now be a collective acceptance of each other, building with our common light.

We will all meet at various crossroads and enjoy our moments together.

Remember that it is not the destination, but joining each end with a new beginning.

It is not an individual task for you alone, but rather a deprogramming of each of us from the illusion of separation.

We will not all be physically close, but we will be bonded across all dimensions by our love.

It is time for each of us to redefine the truth of love that we personally feel is the strongest.

Currently we spend a lot of our time regurgitating memorable moments from the propaganda machines.

As if somehow this brings us closer together.

But really this is the equivalent to making small talk about the weather with strangers in an elevator.

Are we passing the time together or doing time alone?

Ah hell, the sun's out so let's just enjoy the day, right?

Sure thing, I'll try really hard to forget about the end results of our apathy.

Yup that's a nice fucking sunset alright.

Or how about I wear a button and a flower to show just how much I care about those who are dying from cancer.

Yup that'll sure fix the situation.

Maybe I should wave the flag or tie on a ribbon to support another corporate war.

Does anyone in the audience really believe that the path which we are on will lead us to a good end?

Play out the tape and try to be honest.

That's h, o, n, e, s, t... look it up.

And once that obvious conclusion is reached then we need to find alternative strategies.

Let's pass the suggestion box shall we?

Great we have some really helpful suggestions here, in no particular order:

1) Kill them all and let god sort it out.

Not very original, but we'll add it to the list anyway.

2) Pray hard for some divine intervention.

Again, one of the old stand-bys.

3) Follow a strong leader who tells us reassuring things, like we are better that the rest.

We sure have a *great* history with that one.

4) Put the women in charge.

Definitely gonna put a star beside that one, but still pretty vague.

5) Open up the current system with complete transparency.

Love it, definitely see some potential there.

6) Eat the rich.

One of my personal favorites.

Will Steven Tyler please stand up.

7) Fire bomb any and all corporations deemed responsible for the current economic situation.

Far too much collateral damage including environmental pollution.

8) What would Hitler do?

WTF?! Who let Donald Trump in here?

9) Let the various races battle to the death, there can be only one.

Right, because might is right and certainly there wouldn't be any problems if we were all the same color. Not!

10) Ignore those problems, after all they are beyond our control.
Okay, first thing is that I have to ask whether you have even tried to understand the situation?
Do you really believe that none of this impacts your life or the lives of your loved ones?
And if you believe that then you certainly *don't* understand the situation.
Just out of curiousity, I would be interested to know how much money is spent globally on disinformation and wet work to silence the dissent?
But not to worry my friends, that shit only works when we are unaware of the enemy's tools and intentions.
We are. We will. We care. We do.
So think of yourself as a color, and join the rainbow.
Consider this.
Do you create the sun and the rain or are we all one and the same?
It is all happening at the same time.
There is no dread, since it is neither in the past or the future.
All that pesky negativity is like the annoying student doodling on the desk next to you.
It is only your problem if you choose to sit there.
But you chose this perspective to experience, so do it.
Or don't, but it won't be for lack of opportunity.
Returning to the list, I'm not convinced that there needs to be a particular order for the accumulation of positive acheivements.
The most important thing above all is to follow your heart.
We are now like that child back in the day who fell into the well.
All we can see now is the light out.
We have gone down so far on so many different levels that there are only two choices left.
Give up or fly.
So do you want to give up the life which you have led up until now?
Or would you like to give it some meaning?
The biggest thing to remember is that we are never ever alone.

Bold And Brightest

So here we are, still waiting...

Do they still teach WW2 history in school?

What did the Allies fight for anyway?

Today's dirty, selfish, bullshit societies?

This constant variety of rotating wars?

Nonstop political attacks, globally, regionally, psychologically, and physically.

Religious upheavals everywhere, including the persecution of the religious by the atheists, agnostics, etc.

Class warfare from the top, bottom, and middle which constantly morphs and evolves to seem fresh and new each time.

The age old battle of the sexes, which as a man I can truly only partially understand.

Grievances which generations have for each other, believing the others don't understand.

Cultural intolerances, usually with the majority persecuting the minority followed by the inevitable minority attempted backlash.

There are so many others.

And there are numerous solutions.

But I suppose the biggest questions being...

Do you give a fuck?

Does anyone else?

Are enough people interested in making the necessary changes?

And what are those changes specifically?

Well now, maybe we should backup a little bit first and spend some time doing an indepth analysis of what's really going on.

You see, one of the most powerful and prolific tools used to either set off or perpetuate these conflicts is to control the information available to the mass public. Then use *leaked* info to create a single point of outrage directed in the desired direction.

This is used so often and in so many areas that even if a single individual delves deeper into the facts, others are so busy with their personally tailored outrage that they barely notice let alone have the time to incorporate this *new* info into their perspective.

And perspective is a major obstacle to our unity as *humanitarians*.

A historical era which needs more accurate analysis is the protest groups of the 60's and 70's.

Whether that be the antiwar, civil rights, or various other movements.

The one thing that many of these larger movements had which today's so-called causes lack were credible, knowledgeable, and powerful leaders.

And now for one of those topics which the average person will either shrug off or even audibly laugh at out loud.

You see, in the world of today's sprawling corporatocrasy with its tentacles reaching into every aspect of our society.

There have been numerous well meaning leaders who have tried to help.

But in order to combat the global ignorance of a certain situation, one needs to educate the others in order to gain a *common* understanding.

And in order to spread these ideas you need access to a *vehicle of propaganda*.

But in the growing corporate and government monopolies all the most useful standard methods of information media (books, television, radio, etc) have either been bought out or squashed.

Therefore many well-intentioned *leaders* have tried to be more creative in their approaches, with various results.

And the ones who started to gain momentum and possibly effect a change or two have been simply eliminated.

Pause for ignorant laughter and ridicule...

But what to do if this *is* true?

In many ways it reminds me of the stories related by the survivors of the Nazi occupation of Europe.

Initially during the first wave of the takeover, some brave souls will try to stand up and protect the persecuted.

But when the negative force is too strong to begin with then the best and brightest are mostly taken out in the beginning.

Then the period of long suffering starts, where a leaderless resistance begins to organize in secret.

Slowly gaining the strength, size, and talent necessary to carry out the unwelcomed tasks in this crucial time.

A razor's edge balance between the appearance of apathetic inaction and fanatical overreacting.

Most important of all is to continue to grow the support and love for the *ultimate ideal*.

Returning to a civilized world community self-governed by a rainbow of equality.

The hardest part during this struggle being trying not to lash out at the constant *evil* actions of the oppressors.

Knowing that eventually we will have to band together in a decisive rebellion.

It is fucking insanity on all sides.

However that is an aging comparison and the situation today has many underlying similarities, but more than not it is a whole new monster.

Thankfully we have an unstoppable multigeneration of beautiful minds.

Since we are also the creative force behind most good art and science, we will right these wrongs in time.

At present there are many tools of control which are being used to rob us of our privacy and individuality.

Oh sure they are sold to us in packages which appear to be needed and usually seem quit logical.

But that is because, as always, in this advertising nightmare we are *sold the sizzle* or rather the explosion.

Like it has been said so often, follow the money and power to find who really benefits.

Where did the weapons come from?

What is the honest answer as to why a conflict was inevitable?

I mean really, when was the last time that a western leader stepped up and admitted that not only were these tribulations expected, but many were actually encouraged?

Compartmentalization with detached (on so many levels) oversight.

We live at a time where the majority of investment is in ways to make more money.

Look at city infrastructure, education, health *care*, etc.

Those are situations which require the knowledge and contributions of those most effected.

But in our corporate, double-wide, hellscape those making the crucial decisions aren't even close to understanding let alone caring about this *common people's* environment.

Divide and conquer or more accurately *divide and rule.*

As has been said by many over the years, we were conquered long ago.

So let's not get caught up in the divisive tools used to separate the religions, races, sexes, ages, etc.

For a long time on this planet, the only real distinction that matters to myself, my friends, and probably you...

The masters vs the slaves.

Most of the 99% understand this on some level of their consciousness.

But the top 4% of this 99% (approximately) have sold us out for various selfish reasons.

And we listen!

Ministry Of Truth

So what the hell do you want out of this life anyway?
Do you even know, did you ever?
Are you content to be blind, deaf, and dumb?
They say it takes all kinds to make the world work.
And I try to be non-judgmental and accepting of most of it.
But I am currently human and just this side of perfect ;)
So there are a couple of things which I can't abide, so long as I have a say.
Hurting others is a big no no.
It is said that ignorance of the law is no excuse.
And I would say that we should try to understand how our actions affect others.
In tension.
Earth, the biggest stage ever.
Be honoured just to have a small part to play.
And when there is an opportunity for more, go for love.
All else is less.
Beyond wanting, beyond those cultivated thoughts which if you really examine them, didn't originate with this personae that is you.
Aiming for those needs, beyond the individual outcome.
Streamline and eliminate those actions, thoughts, and unintentional influences on others which aren't our most positive versions of this reality.
At some point everyone should spend a prolonged period questioning the foundations of their reality.
But before you go into the desert to do peyote, what I am really talking about is our cultural, political, emotional, physical environment etc.
Because I suppose what is one of the most frustrating issues for me is when I see others following their brainwashed programming.
Many of you probably know what I mean.
Most of us can get along and have pleasant surface conversations.
But when we stray into topics which don't follow mainstream dogma/ propaganda, then those indoctrinated begin to behave like malfunctioning androids.
Does not compute, does no compute...
I've been on that side of the perspective and not only do I sympathize and

empathize, but I try to help with the de/re-programming.

Alas the frustration in these scenarios is caused by the futility of liberating people one at a time, and the time that takes...

Only to have them understand most of the necessary material and become completely overwhelmed, shut down, and then resume the same old same old.

Meanwhile the big state media disinformation/ignorance machinery programs millions a day with what they are supposed to want and care about.

You know the drill, like when those who saw what was going to happen in Nazi Germany before it reached critical mass.

Or trying to convince a western culture indoctrinated into Christianity that Armageddon is most definitely not a certainty but is now in danger of becoming a tragic self-fulfilling prophecy.

But never lose hope my friends, one individual or a small group can make a huge difference.

There is a great character in Asimov's Foundation series called The Mule who defied all conventional understanding and radically changed the course of history.

My point is that we need to find ways of defying the darkening inertia which is enveloping us.

So many questions and possible choices.

Do we try the separation movement where we, in one form or another, remove ourselves and our loved ones from the *evil* in this society?

Do we struggle against the torrent of this river as it flows ever closer to the waterfall?

How long can we sustain the effort?

Do we do a little of both, or nothing at all?

Maybe I should just admit that I don't have all the answers.

But really, more people need to recognize that there is a huge hole in the soul of our society.

Which is another of those contrary propaganda pictures which are constantly presented to us on TV, in most movies and magazines, etc.

The idea of the *happy shiny* families who go to school/work, pay their taxes, take vacations to Disneyland, and generally don't rock the boat.

But the actors and models look so happy and the corporations are constantly emphasizing that they are trying to make our lives easier.

Meanwhile, the *intelligence* agencies admit that one of the biggest problems in their ability to recruit the *best and brightest* is that they have already been snatched up by Wall Street and Silicon Valley.

I would also point out that many of our most talented artists have been lured into the easy money of corporate advertising.

Which are the opposite targets for the armed forces recruiters who prey on the poor and vulnerable.

Once again, each of these capitalist pigeon holes have their fine print which hold the carrot of achievement forever out of reach.

Until either a *preventable* illness or *old* age eventually takes it all away from them with none of their legacy left behind.

So where are we now?

Of course we all know that beyond time and our physical constraints, we are all one.

But *we* all chose to give this Earth-bound experience a try.

And I am fairly certain that when we *individually* decided to incarnate, that it wasn't for a vacation or for the chance to torture each other.

That would certainly be a huge waste of an opportunity.

One thing that I do know for sure is that most of our fellow humans have suffered multiple serious traumas which have massively impacted their lives.

"*Psychological Trauma*, a type of damage to the mind that occurs as a result of a severely distressing event. Trauma is often the result of an overwhelming amount of stress that exceeds one's ability to cope or integrate the emotions involved with that experience."

And there are many other types of trauma.

My point here is that these events and scars alter those involved and steer them off a *normal* healthy path to growth.

I am curious where we could end up with a generation of healthy individuals in mind, body, and soul.

Imagine in twenty years if we could develop methods of recycling or transforming all of the worst pollutants into something safe and beneficial.

Or if we could make the weapons of war pointless and archaic.

And mood altering substances redundant.

Basically reprogram the global game.

Maybe upgrade from Windows 10 to Portals 20.

We now have virtual reality where people are free to do anything without physically hurting others.

So the old arguments about how we don't have the right to tell others how to live becomes easier to accommodate.

Another example from the area that I live is the idea of switching our voting system from the traditional first past the post format.

We will have a referendum to decide if we wish to switch to a form of Proportional Representation.

It is a somewhat complex discussion, but certainly worth investigating.

Ultimately what we are trying for is transparency and cooperation in the governments which *we* have bought and paid for.

And while we are talking about decency, how about rebooting the corporations and installing an updated antivirus in their boardrooms to eliminate these greedy tapeworms we call CEOs.

Then as we continue to balance the scales in favour of compassion and justice in economics, we can once again afford an education system which will train the next generation to value clean air and water.

Not only that, but also give them the freedom and creativity to correct many years of neglect and pollution.

There are so many deeply disturbing and controlling aspects of our current environment.

For example, consider the areas and venues which are available to our youth free of charge in openly creative environments.

There aren't many, and there are numerous reasons for this.

Mostly, if we dig deep enough and try to be objective, to do with how profoundly sick and selfish our capitalism has become.

And when we do have functions run by supposedly *charitable* organizations, we very often find that a religious or financial interest is the overriding organizing principle with distorted agendas.

And don't get me started on the rampant paedophilia which is lurking like a Catholic priest.

Also the unnatural social interactions setup by bars, pubs, nightclubs, raves, concerts, etc.

Yup, sounds pretty grim indeed.

But I am simply pointing out the holes in the wall which need to be filled and painted over.

Obviously people have the right to do as they choose provided that they don't negatively affect others.

But currently the social environment is a pay-per-play system riddled with pyramid schemes, addictions, brain-washing indoctrinations, and on...

It really makes me sick that when we are given examples in movies or TV of the histories of our societies *idols* much of the time that person is shown being creative by *letting their hair down* while getting drunk or high.

What a pitiful mind fuck.

Which reminds me, let's give the *airwaves* back to the people.

How completely suicidal is it that our most powerful expressions of art are controlled by groups who's sole overarching directive is to make financial profits.

It seems like the integrity of most of the older large organizations was a bell curve which has run its course and is now bottomed out the far side into a flatline.

Up here in Canuckistan we are definitely heading in the right direction.

Meanwhile down in Amerikkka, who the hell knows when a state of martial law will finally be implemented so that the *undesireables* can be eliminated with a quick and efficient genocide.

Once again we can look back to some of the encouraging recent events.

Like the famous headlines with Harvey Weinstein, Kevin Spacey, etc where some headway is made and they are asked to step down or away from their careers.

But will any of the big ones really see jail time? Doubtful.

And sure Michael Moore is still free to make a great documentary film exposing some poignant truths about the Flint water crises, political deceptions, etc.

But most of those who actually watch are already the good guys and gals.

And just a side note here but when the fascist takeover goes into full swing, the financial record of your ticket to Mike's film will trigger a big red flag in 1984's Ministry of Truth.

Just saying.

All power to the people.

Beating Around The Bush

Right then, I was recently reminded of the enormous scope of our environment.

No I didn't visit the Grand Canyon, Mount Everest, or the Great Pyramid in Giza.

I came across and binge-watched the first season of a great video series called Deep Space.

Up until that point, I have recently been quite wrapped up in the emotions and politics of our current Earthly sit-u-ation.

Just like it is easy to get entangled and distracted by workplace politics.

But I have to take it easy on myself and you all out there.

The really important and downright critical things about the *the big picture* have been heavily suppressed on multiple levels.

Believe it my friends.

I mean most of what I have talked to you guys about up until now has been prologue.

So let's dive right in shall we?

There are incredibly selfish and traitorous reasons why we are lied to about our true origins, our true potentials, and who the hell is zipping around our skies and oceans in saucers, etc.

Give yourself some credit for even finding this little candle of information.

These days, when some decent quality truth about these topics gets out into the wilds of the general population...

Of course, first there are attempts at suppression, so for example if important high quality info is posted on a webpage...

And if that page can't be easily removed, then various techniques are used to block the average user's searching and/or access to said page.

So that even if the info is technically available, no one can find it.

But let's say that the truth gets out and takes hold before normal suppression techniques can prevent it.

Stage two is ridicule, harassment, and an onslaught of disinformation.

So that even though the original ideas can be searched for and found...

Now those search results are teaming with dozens of other semifactual doctored and professional looking competing articles.

And these are littered with various jabs of ridicule at some of the actual most important points and facts from the original *true* post.

Then if the true story continues to gain traction and let's suppose that a large part of the respectability of said story relies on the credibility of the author, then stage three goes into action.

Stage three is the nightmare scenario for an average citizen.

The author is threatened, blackmailed, physically intimidated, etc.

Until they either give in and recant the truth, or they buckle under the pressure to them and their families by ending their life and perhaps their family members as well.

Following this, regardless of whether a suicide note is left with a genuine explanation, this is also swallowed up by the propaganda machine until only the author's close friends and family still believe in the integrity of the person and their original post.

Now I'm getting depressed.

But I know what you are thinking.

Stop beating around the bush and just tell us what we need to know.

Okay so don't quote me on the specifics, but off the top of my head, here goes:

Well obviously not only has humanity made contact with both terrestrial and extraterrestrial non-human entities.

But also that contact was made so long ago that no one really knows anymore when first contact even happened.

And that it isn't just one species but a multitude of *the good, the bad, and the indifferent.*

Now there are a number of reasons given by different individuals and groups for why we little commoners need to be kept ignorant.

Most of us, who have looked into UFOs before, have heard of the Brookings Report.

The big point made about the *findings* in the final report is the idea that the general population would react unexpectedly to the worldwide disclosure of actual extraterrestrial life.

And that it isn't on some far off planet, but all around us and has been for quite some time.

Now personally, I am not too worried about our reaction.

And I think the real reason for suppression of the truth is the fear by those in power of losing their iron grip on our economics, spirituality, health, etc.

Sure, there are both good and bad personalities in all groups.

But in a similar way that the underground drug trade has produced a vile environment for those involved on all levels...

A similar result has occurred in our political, economic, and religious institutions.

So that we have seen recently the veil being lifted off of various negative situations.

Things like racial profiling, sex abuses, banksters, pollution, etc.

Sure there are a multitude of crimes that we humans can blame each other for, and justifiably so.

But I still argue that the larger lies which are perpetrated by the elites (for want of a better term) are far more disastrous to our civilization, planet, solar system, etc.

And like the Americans said back in the day, *I hold these truths to be self evident.*

On so many levels, we are being dumbed-down and distracted.

However, I remind myself and you all out there that these *baddies* aren't even close to a majority.

In fact, part of the reason for their drastic action is because of their fearful minority.

The last 70 years or so since the end of WW2 has been a royal mind-fuck.

Much of this has been fueled by the massive amounts of wealth and technology stolen from others materially, psychologically, spiritually, etc.

So when someone says that we are being lied to by the corporations, politicians, priests, etc.

Then I would suggest that they look progressively up the hierarchy to see who's pulling the strings, but also recognize that following the money will only lead so far.

I know this may come as a shock (he said sarcastically), but money isn't everything.

Okay that's enough background for now, let's turn the page, take a deep breath, maybe a hug, and then compassionately talk about how we can each do something to help.

Obviously, to write down a list of actions, targets, goals, etc would tip our hand to those monitoring these interactions and communications.

As always search your soul and err on the side of love.

Plan See

So I don't want to get off on a rant here but...

Have you ever noticed that however supposedly progressive a film, TV show, book, song, etc tries to be in our western culture.

Whether it is acceptance of minorities or marginalized individuals, which is getting somewhat better, but that is also due to the will of the people.

However, the topics of major political or financial reform or even downright revolution are either conspicuously absent or if the issues are raised then they are presented as the demented fanciful thoughts of people whom you wouldn't for a moment turn your back on.

Whether it is History Channel's demonizing of national leaders around the world who dared to try and achieve independence from the USA Petro Dollar.

Or the presentation in films of revolutionaries from the 60's and 70's as crazy motherfuckers.

But nevermind that, enjoy the car chases, special effects, and pandering humour.

Do you think maybe it has something to do with who really owns and runs the movie studios, TV stations, newspapers, publishing houses, etc.

Obviously, and I wouldn't be so pissed off if it wasn't such an in your face insult.

It's exactly like George Orwell's idea of double think, knowing that something is untrue but tolerating it out of fear.

Fear of what you say?

Okay maybe not you then (ya right), but most people have been manipulated into the life they currently *enjoy*.

Advertising, schools, religion, etc.

My friends, we know it is true!

But it seems like we are in a two level society, and I am not just bitching about the absurd gap that is continuing to widen between the 1% and the rest of us.

No it gets back to the idea that you will know who is really in power by looking at who we aren't allowed to criticize.

Okay now, is everybody in?

Good, now the topic tonight is how do we in the pursuit of an honest and loving humanity go about awakening and deprogramming the rest?

I mean so long as we continue to finance the propaganda of those who are literally controlling and killing us.

Most of us know most of the story but for various reasons we *play by the rules.*

Rule 1, Don't question their authority!

Rule 2, Accept that in order to participate in this society you will need money, lot's of money!

Rule 3, Agree to hand over your children to the current propaganda curriculum, i.e. schools, churches, sports, etc.

Rule Infinity, Accept that you are small and insignificant.

You get the point.

So the big question then is what can we do about it individually and collectively?

The answer generally is be yourself completely.

Don't let anyone else mould or shape who you want to be.

Be honest and critical in determining not only who you should be, but also the persons and environments which you will allow to influence your life.

I totally realize that these ideas are harder to adhere to in reality than in theory.

Most of us currently exist in situations where we have to compromise many times a day.

Hell, most of our employment situations are paying us daily to give up pieces of our soul.

But like the cow going down the chute to its slaughter, we all have very limited options presented.

And those who have a conscience and children would love to have a larger role in educating their children, but kids are expensive and most of the waking time is spent by the adults selling themselves just to maintain the basics.

What starts off as an attempt to *get it right* and not *be like our parents*, ends up with brief moments of *face time* and deprogramming while at the same time being careful not to say anything which would be innocently reported to *The High Command*.

So getting back to us separately and together positively influencing our lives and environment, here is an idea to start with.

We need to eliminate (or at least greatly reduce) the environments of fear.

So that should be easy right?

But like many have said before, including myself, aim for the major players.

Big business, big pharma, big dogma, big oil, etc.

You know, those with unlimited budgets and an interest in keeping things as they are.

It doesn't really matter at this point what their motivations are in these situations.

These out-of-control structures and all their flaws must simply be removed from the situation.

But hold on for a second here, I am not advocating or even suggesting violence in any form.

I know that *we* have grown up with all of this shit from our societies major players.

And I also know that *they* have grown up from common pieces of the whole into monopolies.

Ultimately they are not sentient beings but rather festering tumours which are sucking the *life* out of life.

There was a time in our history when they didn't exist and hopefully we can find a peaceful way to remove them.

Much the same way that some cleaver people are finding ways of eliminating that huge floating mass of plastic floating around in the oceans.

Perspective is key in this reality.

Now the fun part for each of us, remember that we all chose to be here and we also get to choose how and if we will participate.

So my friends, let's spend less time letting the clown's entertain us and more time going to sleep each night with a smile from our positive accomplishments.

Tap into the creative you that best fits each situation and, as much as possible, do this good stuff in the open.

Thus providing examples and encouragement for others.

You see, at this point most of the multitude of people who give a shit are discouraged from even dwelling on a course of positive action.

This is for various reasons, from the numerous examples of others' futile actions, to the fear of actually succeeding in some small way and then getting hammered like the lone nail sticking out of the board.

However as those discouragements and fears are lessened and/or eliminated, then more of our fellow *regular* brothers and sisters will begin to test the waters of realignment for themselves.

And once they get a taste for how good it feels to *level up* in the really real world as apposed to some video game, well then that is a whole new and far more satisfying feeling.

Followed by the yearning to share their experience with their friends and this begins to snowball towards a critical mass of common creation.

That sounds pretty awesome, yes?

But now time for some healthy knowledge and precautions.

As I have been reminded recently, humanity and its commonly observed three dimensional adventure on Earth is also affected by outside and inside influences.

And this is where it gets really strange and complicated.

Here we have the spectrum of players with their own agendas.

However many of those agendas are either positive or neutral towards us *good* people.

And there are those who actually want us to either come to a bad end or at least hold us down in the wars and chaos which are so common in recent history.

So here is something really important to consider.

Those all which I have just alluded to are in many ways far more advanced than us.

So that it can be interpreted that in the past many of our fellow citizens may have been either led astray or even helped.

But my point is that we are so spiritually and cosmically inexperienced that we need to be cautiously but collectively engaged with increasingly open and perceptive determination.

After all, many of us have been yearning for *contact, disclosure*, etc.

And that sounds mostly fun and exciting, but if we think about the effects of long term future interactions, are we really ready for this powerful bag of changes?

This is truly the most profound question of our generation.

So I would suggest that you all pause and not only consider it personally but also discuss with some close friends and really take an honest and objective view of what our short and long-term future could and should be.

Let's call this one Plan See.

Definitely Maybe

So if you really think about it, in order for humanity to truly make it to the next level in every way that you can imagine...

And there most of you go waiting for dumbed-down instructions in between commercial breaks.

Ah, there's the rub.

Go back over the past hundred odd pages and recognize that the adversary is not benign, imaginary, obvious, etc.

But rather, and this is a bold but also controversial point, the greatest threat to potential global peace since the Nazi era.

If you look beyond *traditional* history you will recognize that the efforts involving our enslavement are ages old.

Taking into account the many ancient runs at civilization, like before *the flood* etc.

Now because we don't have much of a traditional record for these past times (i.e. books, films, Facebook memes), I will simply generalize.

There are stories like the Tower of Babel, the fall of Atlantis, the biblical flood, etc.

There are also legends of cataclysms from various causes which could be *logically* attributed to things like asteroids, pole shifts, giant volcanoes, etc.

There are allusions to the state of humanity during these times and possibly the reasons for some of these *incidents*.

And when you consider all these past situations, it can be somewhat depressing.

However it also suggests three possible scenarios for dealing with our current situation.

The white, the black, and the grey.

Obviously the grey (or the fog) is where most of us live.

The black (or evil) is where most of the 1% spend their time.

And the white (or truth) is where those who want peace and love aspire to be.

Once again I will state clearly that I don't claim to know the *mind of god* and as far as I know I am not in contact with any *angels* or *demons*.

The long and short of it is that my life has given me a fairly unique and somewhat privileged perspective.

For some reason I have felt the need to understand our human situation and try to help as best I can.

Now I don't want to bore you to tears with this testimonial shite, but a little clarification might be useful in the future for both of us.

When I say that I have tried to help, I am no *Christ-like* figure who stops to bless and assist everyone I see daily in need.

But I have nothing against those who try that path.

I will say that I have given coins to those with their hands out.

And I briefly did some volunteering with all the *right* motives.

However, the more that I see of our current civilization from the inside and the more info reported by genuine insiders that I digest in an attempt at objective knowledge.

Well then, here we are now.

And yes it is quite bleak at times.

It can be fucking overwhelming.

But please keep in mind that although the *Bond Villains* amongst us would either slaughter or enslave us all if they were given half a chance.

That hasn't happened yet.

And yes it does appear that we are being poisoned, lobotomized, sterilized, and distracted more and more each day.

But that is mostly the corporate banking fascist faction doing whatever they can get away with.

There are also many more with an eye towards long-term cooperation and *positive* evolution.

So I still maintain that we can and should continue to be our true selves in spite of the bastards.

It has served me well for the most part.

But being in the minority is never easy and can be a negative experience at times, so suit up and be prepared for an uphill battle.

There is currently and perhaps will always be both the positive and negative, dark and light, good and evil, etc.

At least on this planet.

Some try to convince us that the global drama is a big game whereby the *gods* shuffled the deck of humanity and randomly dealt each of us our lot, just out of curiosity and entertainment.

Others, bogged down in their negative experience, have convinced themselves that this is more like *Hell* and that any chance of improvement is an illusion.

Still others try for the *Paradise on Earth* scenario hoping to re-form those who haven't bought their program yet.

And on, and on, and on...

But by and large the majority of the current generation have been sold a custom tailored apathy.

Information distraction overload, real fake news, and a terrible lack of free time.

After all, why try to change our situation if we aren't even sure what the hell is going on?

Best to just stock up on supplies, keep our loved ones close, and make sure our health insurance is paid up, right?

Well of course we all have our own free will and apathy is currently a popular default position.

Personally having seen behind the curtain, that lifestyle bores me.

But what do I really expect to accomplish anyway, little old me?

I guess a quick and simple answer is that I hope to help us to become we.

Like I have said many times before, it is all about intention.

My best times began when I learned to try and stop lying to myself in all aspects of my life.

From my perspective when I see a negative person who is trying to appear to be decent to others, that is pretty sad.

But at least the thugs and others who are committed to their roles have embraced their intentions.

There are all of us with our individual fears flying around us like agitating demons prodding us to take actions which are truly out of our normal or best characters.

Consider the current western prevalence with drugging its citizens, in all forms and too many negative side effects to name.

The result being a psychological divide and conquer campaign which has left us passive, isolated, and easily distracted.

This battle has been decisively won by the adversary, but the war...

So here's another perspective to empower us my friends.

How about divine intervention?

No I'm not talking about buying our freedom from some religion.

What I am speaking of is seriously considering the multitude of unexplained phenomenon (UFOs, angels, premonitions, etc).

With so many events happening in just the last century, if only a small percentage are factual events, then that certainly does open up what would be considered by the adversary to be a Pandora's Box of knowledge, tools, allies, etc.

No wonder that the mainstream religions and technologists have been either bought out or destroyed by the *corporations*.

There are of course numerous books, videos, radio shows, etc which discuss these topics.

And it is easy to get confused in the overwhelming amount of conflicting information, testimonials, *experts*, and those who *swear* to be telling the truth.

But if you are looking for a great objective book, then I recommend *Alien Agenda* by Jim Marrs.

One of the ideas which I find to be really telling and true to the current and past encounters and trends is the idea that there are in fact non-human beings which are in a tug-of-war for the fate of this planet.

The basic idea being that one side wants to take over Earth to either control us or else take it for themselves.

While the rival faction is in favour of keeping us humans in a state of normal *evolution*, at least as normal as possible given our circumstances.

And then of course there is the rest of the galaxy which is for the most part observing but not interfering.

So that leaves us in a bit of a powerless situation, or at least greatly reduced as far as controlling our own fate.

Either way it sure is a hell of a lot to digest.

But I certainly don't agree with the current *ignorance is bliss* party line which knowingly keeps the general population in the dark by those who are really running the overarching global agendas.

Which on a side note, reminds me of a common theme which has come up many times and makes me curious.

There have been times too numerous to remember when I would be discussing the ideas about dark projects, shadow governments, nefarious corporate agendas, etc.

And of course those who are alluded to being in control are generally called *they*.

Then very casually the person with whom I am conversing will ask who are these *they* to which I have referred.

It could just be my good old paranoia or over-active imagination, but I sometimes feel the fear and anxiety in the way some of them ask and then the way that they anxiously wait for my reply.

It reminds me of an old Russian science fiction book that I read back in the day, called *Definitely Maybe*.

The idea of the book was that a scientist came really close to a revolutionary break through, but that the closer that he got to finishing it, the more chaotic his life became as though *the powers that be* were somehow interfering.

So as has been said numerous times in the past, the question of our generation is what are we willing to fight for and how do we organize the real revolution?